Get Your Head In The Game

The Power Of Positive Mental Attitude

Barb Chrysler

NANSHE
PUBLISHING

Copyright © 2015 Nanshe Publishing
All rights reserved, including the right to reproduce this book or portions thereof in any form whatsoever.

The quotes used were sourced from interviews and material referenced at the back of this book.

Nanshe Publishing

PO Box 20111 Pioneer Park, 123 Pioneer Drive, Kitchener, ON, Canada N2P 1L9

www.nanshepublishing.biz

ISBN: 978-0-9948049-1-4

For every 500 books printed 30 trees will be donated to Tree Canada for reforestation in areas most needed.

Acknowledgements

Thank you to the following people for their contributions to this book.

Book Title – Josh Chrysler, Canada
Cover Model – Josh Chrysler, Canada
Back Cover Model – Philip Grammenos, Canada
Front & Back Cover Photos -
Paul Prachuk, Ukraine
p.prachuk@gmail.com
Book Cover Design – Subrato Deb, India
sddesigns12@gmail.com
Profile Photo – Michael Messner, Canada
mary@artistic-photo.com
Research Assistance
Carlos Pedraza Vázquez, Mexico
charlillo2097@me.com
Esinkuma Sambo, Nigeria
Editor - Richard Nicol, Canada
Editor rnicol999@gmail.com
Nandita Roy, India
roynandita5@gmail.com
Book Reviews
Ainsley Thorne, Chloe Chaumont, Didler Liango
Nelson Velez www.mysocceracademy.co

Dedication

This book is dedicated to Ryan and Josh and the young people I've coached, managed, and watched play soccer and sports.

I hope you realize your dreams.

Table Of Contents

Forward 1

The Power Of Positive Mental Attitude 5
    Follow Your Dream 7
    Believe In Yourself 11
    Make A Commitment 12
    Find Your Purpose 14
    Fulfill Your Destiny 17
    Try Your Best 20
    Be Optimistic 23
    Develop Confidence 25
    Have A Positive Attitude 30
    Find The Right Coach 33
    Strive For A Win 38
    Have Faith 43
    Find Support 47
    Strive To Improve 51
    Enjoy Challenge 55
    Practice On Your Own 57
    Be Willing To Work Hard 66
    Be Willing To Sacrifice 68
    Prepare For The Mental Game 70
    Stay Motivated 72
    Overcome Differences In Ability 74
    Do Not Give Up 75

Play Fair 77
Find Your Passion.. 78
Have Fun.. 84
Work With The Team 85

Inspiring Stories 87
Michelle Akers Practices Things She Does Not Enjoy And Fears 87
David Alaba Plays Fair 89
Pelé Followed His Dream 91
David Beckham Overcomes Adversity 95
Nico Calabria Lets Nothing Stop Him 99
Mia Hamm Works Hard To Improve 102
Zlatan Ibrahimovic Decides His Destiny 106
Philipp Lahm Is A Team Player 112
Lionel Messi Makes Sacrifices 115
Alex Morgan Developed Confidence 118
Ronaldo Overcomes Challenges 119
Manuel Neuer Has A Positive Attitude 122
Arjen Robben Makes The Best Of Life.......... 125
Cristiano Ronaldo Believes In Himself........ 127
Marta Overcomes Barriers............................... 129
Hope Solo Learns From Her Mistakes 131
Robin van Persie Overcomes Failure........... 134
Abby Wambach Eats Well And Focuses On Fitness 138
Sun Wen Believed In Herself When The Coach

Did Not 140
George Weah Has Faith..................................... 142
Zinedine Zidane Helps Others....................... 147

Conclusions 150

Affirmations 152

Author 155

REFERENCES 156

Forward

Participation in sports is an important part of personality and character development in children and youth. Sports can be a whole lot of fun, and can ensure that kids have a balanced physical and emotional life, which makes them great assets to the community as adults. In my experience of running my Soccer Academy for kids in Kissimmee, Florida, I've seen how participation in sports can transform a child's life in multiple ways. It fosters team spirit, respect, integrity, and discipline – all essential qualities.

Barb Chrysler's *Get Your Head in the Game: The Power of Positive Attitude* is a book that promotes fun, fair play, hard work, and sacrifice. It takes the reader into the heads of the masters of soccer, and helps us locate the winning potential in ourselves. It is a great read for children and youths who are interested in soccer, as well as for parents and coaches who want to understand the psychological aspects of sports. Looking at the mental side of the game, it helps youths understand how to believe in themselves, and harness the attitude required to achieve goals. Short biographies of famous players like George Weah, rising from the slums of Africa, to be called to play in Europe at the age of 22 and Lionel Messi, who had a growth hormone illness and was able to overcome this to become a great player; these examples and more help children across the globe understand the importance of positive attitude. The stories illustrate the mental character needed to overcoming adversity and of the importance of believing in your dreams against the odds.

It is an essential read that helps us understand the importance of playing a sport – and how it helps youths deal with emotional and psychological issues that can be overwhelming at a young age. The fun of soccer, combined with the sharp wisdom of this book, makes it a great read for soccer fans and casual readers alike. The lessons that this book imparts are not just applicable in the realm of sports, but the larger and more holistic realm of life itself.

Nelson Velez
Former Pro Player from Colombia, S.A.
Former MLS Player in the United States,
Head Coach and Co-Founder of
My Soccer Academy and CONFUTBO

The Power Of Positive Mental Attitude

You always pass failure on the road to success.
-Wayne Rooney

Successful soccer players believe in themselves; they follow their dreams, many believing that God or a power greater than themselves has given them talent and it is their duty to do justice with it. They are optimistic of creating their own destiny. They keep striving for perfection, learn from their losses, and persevere in the face of challenges. Wanting to be the best they can be, they are not afraid to look deeply within themselves and identify where they need to improve; they train harder, discipline their emotions and make sacrifices. Successful soccer players believe in themselves. They have a passion and love for football, which helps them overcome obstacles. They believe they can do it and to achieve their goal, they train harder and never give up.

This book examines the mental attitude of professional soccer players who have attained elite status. *Get Your Head In The Game* has been organized in an easy-to-understand format for the benefit of both teens and anyone else trying to achieve goals in soccer or any aspect of life. The method used in compiling the content for this book was to read interviews with some of the top soccer players and analyze them, focusing on key themes essential to the achievement of personal dreams. It provides information using the players' voice. Then research was briefly summarized into categories.

Chapter two highlights positive attitudes apparent in the lives of some of the best players in the world. Their stories demonstrate how these soccer players overcame poverty, birth defects, health problems, and other adversities. It is hoped that these stories will motivate young athletes to focus on health and fitness, push their personal limits, and achieve their dreams in soccer and in life. It is a tool, which can be used to help youths stay positive, be confident, and learn the secrets to success. May all your dreams come true.

Follow Your Dream

Anyone who sacrifices his dreams to reality is forever beaten.
-Thomas Müller

Most of the football players mentioned in this book stated that they were following childhood dreams. At a young age, they wanted to be soccer players and pursued that goal. A dream often presents itself as a repetitive thought. And when we are following our dreams, we feel most alive and happy. This book focuses on soccer players who made it to the highest level.

The footballers outlined in this book stand out; they are people who overcame seemingly insurmountable obstacles and went on to achieve their goals. The following pages describe the mental attitude, which helped them accomplish what many just dream of. The quotes below speak of the players' lifelong dreams.

You're obviously conscious of being brash or big-headed, but I always knew I was going to be a footballer when I was seven or eight. I didn't just think I wanted to be one, I knew I was going to be one. Nothing ever surprised me really.
-Michael Owen

I'm a footballer, that's my job and that's all I want to be known for.
-Jamie Redknapp

When I was a child, it was my dream to be a professional footballer. When I was 14, I visited Milan's San Siro Stadium and remember thinking how unbelievable it was. From then onwards, I vowed that one day I would be playing there – and I am very proud that I achieved this and also for everything else I have managed to achieve in football.
-Andriy Shevchenko

I have never imagined doing anything other than football.
-Ronaldinho de Assis Moreira

I've always wanted to be a top footballer since I was young.
-Michael Owen

Pulling on your country's shirt is the greatest honour a footballer can have. It's what I always dreamed of as a kid and I get a buzz every time.
-Wayne Rooney

If you had told me as a young boy I would have played for and won trophies with my boyhood club Manchester United, proudly captained and played for my country over 100 times and lined up some of the biggest clubs in the world, I would have told you it was a fantasy. I'm fortunate to realize those dreams.
-David Beckham

I had years where, I left the house at 7 am in the morning and returned home at 9 pm in the evening, four days a week... On weekends, we had the league games. It was difficult for the family as well, because I was often not at home. It is difficult to get and keep friends who are willing to cope with that... I also had a dream, so I had to give this sacrifice.
-Manuel Neuer

When I was a kid, I always dreamed of winning the World Cup and lifting the trophy. That was my dream and you think about that.
-Philipp Lahm

I'm living a dream I never want to wake up from.
-Cristiano Ronaldo

I'm living my boyhood dream, which was to play for a European club. The fact that it's a huge club like Barcelona makes it a tremendous honour.
-Neymar da Silva Santos

It was a dream for me to be among such players. My dream was coming true.
-Sammy Kuffour

Believe In Yourself

Dream big, because dreams do happen.
-Alex Morgan

It's not enough to have a dream of being a football player; talent and mental attitude are also equally important. Many people have dreams, but they don't believe that they can achieve them. Professional soccer players not only had those dreams, but they also believed that they would one day realize them. While they might have faced obstacles along the way, they also had a sense of optimism or faith in their abilities.

He is as well a little bit air of arrogant you know, but [he] believes that he is the number one, first it comes from the fact that you know you can. Deeply

inside himself he knows that if he wants he can pass anybody.
-Arsene Wenger on Cristiano Ronaldo

Lots of young people have triumphed at United, so why can't it happen to me? I'm not worried that I'm young. It's an incentive to do the best I can.
-Cristiano Ronaldo

Nobody believed in us in 2002. Nobody believed in the National Team… but we knew our potential.
-Cafu (Marcos Evangelista de Morais)

Beckham's unusual. He was desperate to be a footballer. His mind was made up when he was nine or ten. Many kids think that it's beyond them. But you can't succeed without practicing at any sport.
-Bobby Charlton

Make A Commitment

I always thought I wanted to play professionally, and I always knew that to do that I'd have to make a lot of sacrifices. I made sacrifices by leaving Argentina, leaving my family to start a new life. I changed my friends, my people. Everything. But everything I did, I did for football to achieve my dream.

-Lionel Messi

Commitment is a promise you make to yourself to do something, like chasing a dream. Professional soccer players are committed to achieving their goals, and research suggests that their commitment is found to be greater than those who had a similar level of skill, opportunity, and geography but who could not make it to that level (Van Yperen, 2009). Researchers have also found that players who were intrinsically motivated by things like pleasure or fun were more likely to make a commitment to themselves than those who were extrinsically motivated by things like public regard, reward, or money (Garcia-Mas, 2010).

Every single day I wake up and commit myself to becoming a better player.
-Mia Hamm

Find Your Purpose

To participate in bringing Africa and Europe together in terms of football makes me very happy. We have created some spaces for African soccer. We have made African football respected. We have the talent, it's just a case of teaching the disciplines and providing the facilities and I want to stay in the limelight after my career to help other people progress.
-George Weah

In this quote, Weah illustrates his feelings about being an example to young people. Playing soccer allowed him to have a sense of purpose beyond financial and social rewards. Research suggests that having a sense of purpose boosts your motivation to attain your goals (Taylor, 2013). Having a goal in life is important and working towards achieving the goal helps you draw a sense of satisfaction and well being, especially when the aspirations are realized (Taylor, 2013).

Every kid around the world who plays soccer wants to be Pelé. I have a great responsibility to show them not just how to be a soccer player but how to be like a man.
-Pelé

Pelé's craze was such that the ongoing civil war in Nigeria was suspended, when Brazil went to play; a truce was called while the football game was being played.

I want to play soccer because soccer is the only sport, which stopped a war.
-Young soccer player

I love the National Team so much. Representing 190 million Brazilians, it is a big responsibility. It touches me and I'm still feeling it.
-Cafu Marcos Evangelista de Morais

Michael Zigarelli, author of *The Messiah Method*, studied the Messiah College soccer program to understand the team's phenomenal success. They had 472 wins, 31 losses, and 20 ties for a winning percentage of 92 in a ten-year period for both the women's and men's teams. One of the findings determined that having a sense of purpose made the team more successful.

They remain focused on "playing for the name on the front of their jerseys," a higher purpose that prioritizes sportsmanship and character development and "team over individual." More than that, this perspective may actually influence their on-the-field results because it super-charges their work ethic, it encourages smarter, more selfless play, and it builds team unity - the elusive competitive advantage of striving toward a common goal.
-Michael Zigarelli

You've got no chance of reaching the top if you're just playing for money.
-Gary Lineker

Fulfill Your Destiny

When I was at Inter, I had a knee injury that kept me out for two months. It was near the end of the season – we were trying to win the title. I came on at half-time against Parma and scored two goals in a 2-0 win and Inter won the title. You decide your own destiny.
-Zlatan Ibrahimovic

People who have an internal locus of control believe they control their destiny through hard work, personal characteristics, and choices. Alternatively, individuals with an external locus of control think that their future is determined by fate. Those with an internal locus of control believe they are responsible for their own success. People with an external locus of control believe in luck and external influences for determining success. When people have an internal locus of control, they are more likely to participate in actions that they believe will change their situation and they will work hard to attain what is needed to reach a particular goal. Such people work harder and persevere longer in order to achieve their objectives.

Everyone has his own destiny. God has something for everybody and this is what has been chosen for me. It is for God to know why the others are not here. If opportunity comes, you have to take it.
-Sammy Kuffour

Impossible is just a big word thrown around by small men who find it easier to live in the world they've been given than to explore the power they have to change it.
-David Beckham

A Lothar Matthäus will not be defeated by his body, a Lothar Matthäus will decide his fate himself.
-Lothar Matthäus

I have come a long way from here. Football has been good to me. Everyone has their destiny, but you have to make use of the opportunities. I have spent 15 years at the top of my game. It makes me happy. I

love the games. I love scoring goals. But I have always taken it seriously. It is not what the game gives you, it is what you give it. It is what you choose. You've got to work hard and make things happen.
-George Weah

I was born to play football and always want to be doing these things that I am able to do with the ball.
-Zlatan Ibrahimovic

Many of the players, as well as their families, believed they were born to play football or that it was their destiny.

I used to tease the other kids because I played better than them. Then my father said, "Come here. Don't do this with the kids, because God gave you the gift to play football. You didn't do anything. This was a present from God. You have to respect people because it is important to be a good man, a good person. From now on, you must be this example."
-Pelé

It seems that God brought me to Earth with a mission to play soccer.
-Pelé

My father used to say to me, "You were born to play football. You've got a gift for it. But if you don't work at it and you don't practice, then you'll be just like the rest." He was absolutely right, but then again. I was born to play football, just like Beethoven was born to write music and Michelangelo was born to paint.
-Pelé

Try Your Best

I want to be one of the best players around in two or three years' time, to be a decisive footballer.
-Cristiano Ronaldo

Wayne Harrison, Co-Founder of the Soccer Awareness Elite Academy, believes that successful players are intrinsically motivated. They want to be triumphant with a strong inner desire to be successful. These players expect that they will be successful through hard work and they believe they can overcome any challenge given to them. Coaches find people like these easy to work with. For coaches with under-motivated players, the key is to find a way to motivate them and push them to develop a strong work ethic. Self-motivation and a desire to succeed are often factors, which separate the good from the great players. Players who lack intrinsic motivation may not work hard, and will appear to be lazy.

Harrison believes that extrinsic motivation from parents and coaches is not enough to help players lacking intrinsic motivation. Players with motivation do not give up even when they are losing. It's important for a player to take responsibility for his or her behavior and lack of drive, and to discover the intrinsic motivation to want to be the best. It is not the most technically gifted players but the ones with the burning desire to be the best who succeed.

I'm a Mexican player trying to do my best so all the world can look at my country to see good things.
-Javier Hernandez

I could be an example for the youngsters. If I pass away one day, I am happy because I tried to do my best. My sport allowed me to do so much because it's the biggest sport in the world.
-Pele

I work on my weak points to try to prevent injuries and to always be at my best. I look after myself, but it's not like I spend my whole life in the gym.
-Lionel Messi

As a footballer, you always want to test yourself against the best.
-David Beckham

I would be very proud if, one day, I'm held in the same esteem as George Best or Beckham. It's what I'm working hard towards.
-Cristiano Ronaldo

Dr. Bob Rotella, author of *How Champions Think: In Sports and in Life* (2015), wrote about the mindset of players he has worked with and observed. Rotella talks about the importance of setting high goals because they motivate individuals to pursue training, mentorship, and nutrition needed to achieve or surpass average, mediocre achievements.

Whether it's a friendly match, or for points, or a final, or any game – I play the same. I'm always trying to be my best, first for my team, for myself, for the fans, and to try and win.
-Lionel Messi

Be Optimistic

The team is hurt, but we have a great desire to win. There is certainly not a lot of happiness on this team after what happened to us in the last two games, but I'm always an optimist.
-Gianluigi Buffon

Researchers examined the relationship between soccer players' optimism and performance by assessing their shots on goal, goals, fouls, and passes attempted and completed. They found that the performance of pessimistic soccer players varied, depending on the performance of the team. If the team was winning, the players performed well, but if they were losing, the players' performance was not as good. On the other hand, optimistic players tended to play consistently regardless of their team's performance. People with optimistic bent of mind not only try harder, but also perform better in adverse situations (Gordon and Kane, 2001). Optimistic individuals are resilient; they perceive opportunities that pessimistic people do not.

One way to change your view from pessimistic to optimistic is to pay attention to your internal voices and replace the negative thoughts with positive ones. For example, instead of saying, 'I can't pass,' tell yourself, 'I am great at passing and every day, my passing accuracy improves.' Write down daily affirmations and repeat them regularly.

You can learn more from the lows than the highs. The highs are great. But the lows make you really look at things in a different way and want to improve. Every player will have both in their careers, and I have, but what you get is that experience which is so important to perform at your best.
-Wayne Rooney

Every disadvantage has its advantage.
-Johan Cruyff

We'll do it, we'll do it.
-Zinedine Zidane

Develop Confidence

I don't need a captain's band to lead a team to victory.
-Hope Solo

Self-confidence is the athlete's perception that he or she has the ability to compete at a certain level. Research suggests that using imaging may enhance confidence and performance. Imaging is when the players see themselves achieving a goal such as winning against another team; it can be helpful towards one's performance and the development of confidence and mental toughness. Research has shown that the more confident the players were, the more likely they were to use this type of visioning (Munroe-Chandler, Hall, and Fishburne 2008).

You have to be really determined and have really high self-esteem and confidence.
-Marta Vieira da Silva

My confidence comes from the daily grind; training my butt off day in and day out.
-Hope Solo

I was always confident in my own ability. I was determined to become somebody in [the] future.
-Sammy Kuffour

We are capable of reaching the World Cup final.
-Fabio Cannavaro

We'll give them the respect we give all our adversaries, but we are also sure of our own capabilities.
-Luís Figo

Bill Beswick, Sports Psychologist and author of *Focused for Soccer: How to Win the Mental Game*, has discussed the role of confidence in building complete players (2010). *"Although I urge players to take responsibility for building their own self-concept and confidence, every player is influenced, positively or negatively, by the comments received from family and friends, from those who surround them daily"* (Beswick, 2010).

The confidence of both the individual and the team is necessary to be successful at soccer. To face challenges, you must feel confident in your ability to overcome them. Losses and criticism from media and others are a constant assault on player and team confidence. There are two voices within us: the "can do" voice and the "can't do" voice; we choose which one we listen to; thus, the "can do" voice needs to be stronger.

When setbacks occur, the players who can look at themselves assess the situation, take responsibility for it, and work towards correcting it; this builds their confidence. They face their fears, negative perceptions of others, and their mistakes or losses. Setbacks are viewed as obstacles to be overcome. Your reaction to a situation or setback is more important than the obstacle or situation itself. Surround yourself with people who promote your sense of confidence. If you are feeling a lack of confidence in your position, assess the components of that position; it will often give you perspective that while one particular part may be challenging right now, you are doing well in other areas. Players can work on developing their own confidence.

Much of the responsibility for building confidence in the team rests with the coach. Meeting with the team before or after the practice to outline the vision and plan, which will detail where the squad currently stands, where they are going, and how they are going to get there will do much to build confidence. Hard work and training will help the team feel that they are prepared for each game; however, it's important to remember to have fun, as this helps with attitude and energy. Coaches also build confidence by helping the team and individuals to realize their potential. They must see what they can do and not be focused on what they can't do at that particular moment. Players should also be praised. Coaches should be careful not to allow their emotions to interfere with the post-game message they deliver; it should not be one they would regret.

When I go into the game, nothing before the game matters. It is important that we think for 90 minutes with full concentration on the next game.
-Lothar Matthäus

Have A Positive Attitude

I promise I will score more goals at the Stretford End. I'm aware of the statistic and it's time to change it.
-Robin van Persie

Bill Beswick, the team psychologist to the English Premier League and England National Soccer teams, wrote *Focused for Soccer: How to Win the Mental Game* (2010). In it, he discusses three types of players: those born gifted with a good attitude who will succeed unless people get in the way; those born gifted with a bad attitude who will unlikely succeed unless they address their approach; and those born with less talent but a great attitude who will use every opportunity presented and will usually succeed. He defined a good attitude as physical intensity, mental focus, high emotional energy, mental toughness, and resilience. A healthy outlook is developed through repeated attempts to react in a positive way to stress. Elements that influence attitude include personality characteristics (i.e. introverted or extroverted, optimistic or pessimistic), the environment and the people in it (coaches, parents, and excellent facilities for training). Often coaching is the first place to start in the development of a healthy attitude. A coach's attitude can impact on player performance.

In football as in watchmaking, elegance means nothing without rigor and precision.
-Lionel Messi

Italians can't win the game against you, but you can lose the game against the Italians.
-Johan Cruyff

If a team wants to intimidate you physically and you let them, they've won.

-Mia Hamm

For sportsmen or women who want to be champions, the mind can be as important, if not more important than any other part of the body.

-Gary Neville

When coaches are asked about the key to winning a soccer game, they credit 50% of the success to having a winning attitude in their players and team. The balance goes to defensive organization, 10%; attacking organization, 10%; transition organization, 10%; set plays (free kicks), 10%; unique players, 5%; and luck, for example, referees' calls, 5%. The mental game is viewed as the most important component of a win.

Beswick (2010) discussed the importance of making a choice to fight or overcome the obstacle standing in the way of your dreams. Once this decision is made, an individual gains confidence and acceptance of the challenge, and begins to prepare for it. With enthusiasm, high energy, and strength of mind, a person can become strong enough to face and surpass obstacles.

Find The Right Coach

There are things in life, which do not deserve comments. That is something I am not going to talk about for obvious reasons. I always respect my coaches and set out to learn from them. In Portugal, people say: 'I do not spit in the meal I am eating.' So that I prefer to stick to positive things.
-Cristiano Ronaldo in an interview about Jose Mourinho

While no one is perfect, some coaches are better than others at helping you develop a positive attitude. It is sometimes difficult for youths and parents to find a good coach. And what works for one person may not work for another. The following behaviours are indications of an inferior coach.

Coaches who

- humiliate, demean, or use fear as teaching tools;
- say negative or demeaning things in front of other people;
- think winning games is the most important aspect;
- place pressure on injured players to play;
- play favorites;
- instruct young players not to tell their parents what is happening at practice; and,
- treat players with disrespect or allow bullying.

Parents may perceive the coach as inept but the young players may love him as they will see through the bad behavior and believe the coach has their best interests at heart. It's a fine line between learning to work with difficult people and staying in environments, which could potentially destroy your belief in yourself and remove all the fun of playing the game.

Throughout life there will be some people that are challenging to work with in positions of authority, such as your teachers, coaches, or bosses, and they may treat you unfairly for no apparent reason. Working with a difficult coach is an opportunity to learn how to get along with problematic people. Do not embarrass the coach in front of other people. If you want to discuss the issues with him or her, ask for a meeting in private and carefully think about what you want to say.

The coach may just be trying to make you a better player and you could ask him or her what you need to do to improve your game. You may feel the need to tell the coach how his or her behavior is impacting your game. In doing so, you need to choose your words wisely and be prepared for the consequences. Some people can take offence and things may get worse for you. This is not to suggest that they always do. They may also get better, but you will never know until you raise it.

Realize that you need to continue with your dreams and ambitions and find a way to succeed. In larger areas, there may be more opportunities to shop around for a good coach. Try to assess the football coaches before the start of the season – watch games and practices, and talk with other players or parents. Observe the turnover of players on the team and the reasons for that turnover. What do past players say about the coach?

If the problem you're having with your coach is that you are not on the starting line-up, have a discussion with him or her about how you can improve and be willing to work hard to get there. If you don't want to work hard or have an excuse regarding why you can't do, what is being asked then perhaps you can work on improving your attitude. Sometimes people have the tendency to take things for granted. It's a disastrous attitude to have. If you were the star player in grade 7 that does not mean you will retain the star player status in grade 9 too. Every time you move up, you will be required to advance your skillset and put in more work in order to achieve the skills needed to become a more complete player.

You may sometimes feel your coach is disrespecting you and you are finding it hard to tell if it is because you are being too sensitive to honest criticism or that you are being unfairly treated. Ask someone else if they notice that your coach is treating you differently. If others feel the same, then perhaps you may need to address this.

But the coach just decided to really yell at me in front of everyone, and in front of the fans, for really no reason. He wanted to yell at me, and I just told him, like, "Really? You're really just going to yell at me because I'm the youngest player?" All I said was, "You just want to show your power, you know." Like, what's up with that? I didn't cuss him out or anything... That coach got fired. I really don't care about that. I was laughing when he got fired to be honest.

-Bobby Wood

Make an honest attempt to work out the issues with the coach and listen to what he or she has to say. Do not respond in haste. Try to do what the coach says and see if it helps (Oden, 2015). Working with other people requires a good attitude. You can't control them, but you can control your responses.

Strive For A Win

It is better to win ten times 1-0 than to win once 10-0.

-Vahid Halilhodžić

When you have success, you just want to repeat it again and again. It is the best life I can imagine. I want to achieve as much as it is possible to achieve with this team.

-Lionel Messi

Researchers have found that the desire to win was ranked 8 out of 10 in importance for the reason why young people participate in soccer (Seefeldt, Edwing, and Walk, 1992). Darren Treasure, Professor of Sport and Exercise at Arizona State University, recommends that coaches and parents focus on the development of task-orientation goals that encourage skill development and not just winning. Ego-oriented individuals look at success in terms of winning and outperforming others, whereas task-oriented individuals look at skill development. Elite athletes are highly developed in ego and task orientation. They feel successful when they win and outperform others, but they understand that they may not always win and look for other ways to define success and view it as an opportunity to improve their skill.

Sometimes you have to accept you can't win all the time.
-Lionel Messi

Football's not just about scoring goals — it's about winning.
-Alan Shearer

It doesn't matter who scores the goals so long as we win.
-Steven Gerrard

Love of fierce competition becomes an equally important reason to play. This intensity is what sets winners apart as you advance up the ladder of soccer success.
-Mia Hamm

I've never played for a draw in my life.
-Sir Alex Ferguson

Obviously the motivation is to win so when that doesn't happen, you really have to look forward and keep motivated to the next time and just keep at it because it's part of the game.
-Marta Vieira da Silva

I wouldn't have moved if I'd had doubts. Instead, from day one I was almost certain we'd win trophies – not in a couple of years but this year. I saw the players training; I saw the way they behaved, the way they lived, their mentality, the way the staff worked, the way the manager and the staff acted... When all those elements combine you end up with a team of champions. It also helps when you have so many players who know how to win... I could see in everybody's faces how determined they were.
-Robin van Persie, 2013.

At the beginning when I started, everything was fun. I was doing what I wanted to do. Now it's all more serious. You represent a club and you need to win. If you don't get results, someone else comes and takes your place. It is a totally different situation. But I am still here for a couple of years.
-Zlatan Ibrahimovic

I am not that aggressive, despite what people think. I really care about football, and wherever I have been, I have wanted to win trophies. Sometimes when you

care about something so much emotions can get high, but I am a nice guy and I get annoyed when people don't care as much as me.
-Zlatan Ibrahimovic

If you have no motivation to win anymore, then it's time to retire.
-Manuel Neuer

I am competitive and I feel bad when we lose. You can see it in me when we've lost. I'm in a bad way. I don't like to talk to anyone.
-Lionel Messi

Something deep in my character allows me to take the hits, and get on with trying to win.
-Lionel Messi

Every footballer wants to play forever. And if you are going to keep on playing — to enjoy it to the full — you want to win games, and as a result, trophies.
-Ryan Giggs

The more difficult the victory, the greater the happiness in winning.
-Pelé

Have Faith

After the accident I had, many doctors tell me my career was over. Buddhism helped me achieve what I had been hoping for.
-Roberto Baggio

I come from a very Catholic family and my sister is a nun; I pray every day in the morning and in the evening and I always encourage my players to go to mass. I think that by attending mass a team finds better cohesion and serenity. You might lose a match, but you never lose sight of what really counts.
-Giovanni Trapattoni

Jesus is my strength.
-Marcelo Bordon

When I was born, the man in the sky pointed to me and said, 'that is the guy.'
-Romario

God created me to delight people with my goals.
-Romario

Simon Desmarais-Zalob, author of *First, I'd Like to Thank God, An Exploration of the Relationship Between Athletes and Faith*, conducted research on faith and successful sports players. He concluded that while faith is not necessary to become a successful athlete, it can help professional players overcome adversity.

In their book, *Do Hard Things: A Teenage Rebellion Against Low Expectation,* Alex and Brent Harris talk about how to use your God-given gifts, which everyone is born with. They suggest that the key is hard work, which is not promoted as much in this culture where youths have few chores and there is a pervading sense of entitlement.

Young people are often given things without working for them. Their book provides biblical insight and examples to help teens take on responsibility in order to achieve better lives.

The authors discuss:
- stepping outside your comfort zone;
- going beyond what is expected;
- working with others to achieve your goals;
- working on small things that may not provide immediate rewards; and,
- doing hard things that most players do not engage in.

Soccer players have talked about the importance of many people in their lives: their parents, coaches, and mentors. Additionally, many speak of the importance of a higher power. Prior to FIFA banning political and religious messages on shirts, some players wore white shirts under their jerseys and, after scoring a goal, would lift them up, revealing messages such as, "Jesus loves you." Recently, in celebration of the Champions League victory, Barcelona's Neymar wore a headband which said, "100% Jesus."

I collect crucifix necklaces – it's because of my relationship with God. I always had a gift. I was shown the skills and I am a fantastic footballer but I do believe God gave me the gift.
-Cristiano Ronaldo

Of course the work is very, very important. That is exactly what my father meant: God gave you the gift to play football, but this is a present. You must respect people and work hard to be in shape. And I used to train very hard. When the others players went to the beach after training, I was there kicking the ball. Another thing I say is, if I am a good player, if I have a gift from God but I don't have the physical condition to run on the field what am I going to do?
-Pelé

Find Support

The support of family and coaches was viewed as important in helping players to have both practical resources like boots and also providing encouragement. In *Pelé: The Autobiography* (2006), he talks about his disappointment after the 1966 World Cup because the Brazilian team lost and he was injured. He said that the birth of his daughter Kelly Cristina in 1967 helped to remove some of the pressure and bring back his enjoyment of the game. Other players also mentioned that support from family was helpful.

I've always had a great relationship with my two brothers; I have always had their support in my football and in everything. They've been very close to me and we have a great relationship.
-Lionel Messi

I wouldn't have achieved what I have done today without my family. I'm grateful for my parents' sacrifice, which made me realize my dreams. I owe everything to Victoria and the kids, who have given me the inspiration and support to play at the highest level for such a long period.
-David Beckham

Researchers of middle class families found that initially, parents generally provided a supportive function in getting the child involved in sports. They did not emphasize a particular sport but were committed to supporting their child's athletic pursuits, and that as the child aged, they made sacrifices in their lives in order to support their child's dreams.

Parents also focused on creating ideal learning environments for their children. Families often dedicated more resources to child athletes, which sometimes resulted in jealousy and bitterness in siblings (Cote, 1999). Other researchers found that individuals who sought support when they were experiencing problems or setbacks were more likely to reach the level of professional adult soccer players than their equally talented peers. Researchers thought that perhaps the support they received reduced their stress levels, and as a result the players involved in the research may have demonstrated better coping skills (Van Vperen, 2009).

We never had much money, my family never let me give up on my dream. My brother would work to buy me boots. My father would scrape together money for me to take the buses to Gama, a club in the city. But I gave everything. Looking back, all the sacrifices my family and I made, they were all worth it. I always believed, even if I didn't think things would happen so quickly. My brother is proud, too. He told me to be patient when I was not in the team at Tottenham, that my time would come. He's happy for me.
-Sandro Raniere Guimarães Cordeiro

I remember Arsène kept telling me, 'You can be a great player, you can be the best in the world.' I thought he was talking stupid. But I'll always keep trying, I'm telling you. Then came a time when my career was improving and I thought Arsène might be right... What can I pay him? I can't give him cash because he makes money. And money can go but the trophy will stay, to remind him what he did for a player.

-George Weah

Weah gave Arsène Wenger, his coach, his 'World Player of the Year' trophy. The role of family and others who believe in you is helpful when striving to achieve a dream. When examining the role of parents and coaches in the review of quotes, the role of parents varied with some parents being actively involved and making sacrifices, and other parents being not as actively involved. Coaches were also mentioned as having a strong belief in sports being the players' destiny or gift.

Strive To Improve

Every year I try to grow as a player and not get stuck in a rut. I try to improve my game in every way possible. But that trait is not something I've worked on, it's part of me.
-Lionel Messi

The importance of striving to improve performance is critically important to play at the top levels as is evident in research and player interviews. Carol Dweck, author of *Mindset: The New Psychology of Success* (2007), suggests people with a fixed mindset think their talents, ability, and intelligence are stable; this is the mindset that weakens incentive to improve. Individuals with a growth mindset believe that they can improve through training, commitment, and assistance from others. People with a growth mindset stay engrossed and inspired to learn. When individuals with a growth mindset commit errors, they look at how to improve. Individuals who have a growth mindset engage more as the obstacles become more difficult. Dweck's research has shown that mindsets can change from a fixed to a growth mindset with training and by changing one's belief system. Professional soccer players often commented on their desire to learn.

I have many years to get better and better, and that has to be my ambition. The day you think there is no improvements to be made is a sad one for any player.
-Lionel Messi

You cannot allow your desire to be a winner to be diminished by achieving success before and I believe there is room for improvement in every sportsman.
-Lionel Messi

Many people say I'm the best women's soccer player in the world. I don't think so. And because of that, someday I just might be.
-Mia Hamm

My strength is to do the right things: eat good, sleep well, train well and improve myself on football to focus for the football.
-Cristiano Ronaldo

I'm not a perfectionist, but I like to feel that things are done well. More important than that, I feel an endless need to learn, to improve, to evolve, not only to please the coach and the fans, but also to feel satisfied with myself. It is my conviction that there are no limits to learning, and that it can never stop, no matter what our age.
-Cristiano Ronaldo

I learned a long time ago that there is something worse than missing the goal, and that's not pulling the trigger.
-Mia Hamm

I still look at myself and want to improve.
-David Beckham

I always try to watch games I've played in. Like any job, you've got to improve your performance.
-Wayne Rooney

I don't really know what happened. We lost a Champions League semi-final against Manchester United and we lost the league to Real Madrid on goal difference. I don't really know what happened, but at least it served as a lesson to make sure it doesn't happen again.
-Lionel Messi

Every single day I wake up and commit to myself to becoming a better player.
-Mia Hamm

I give 100% of myself to the game and to my training. I'm very determined and really eager to always be great at what I do. I've always been motivated to go further and further and just accomplish more and more.
-Marta Vieira da Silva

To improve a lot; to keep enjoying this dream, because for me it's a dream to be playing here, to keep improving and keep learning, to help my teammates with all my effort and all my work, and of course to win trophies.
-Javier Hernandez

Whatever happens, there are always things you could have done better. You score two goals and you usually feel you could have done better. You score two goals and you usually feel you could have scored a third. That's perfectionism. That's what makes you progress in life.
-Eric Cantona

Enjoy Challenge

All my life I've been playing up, meaning I've challenged myself by competing with players older, bigger, more skillful, more experienced – in short, better than me... At ten, I eventually joined an eleven-year-old-boy's team and, eventually, led them in scoring.
-Mia Hamm

I think it's my personality to overcome things, learn from them and become stronger, both personally and professionally. To be honest, I welcome those hardships.

-Hope Solo

I'm inspired by challenges. My life was always like this. When things are really good, really easy it's not cool for me. There is something lacking inside of me, I need some prick to turn up being rude about me. This makes me give something extra.

-Romário de Souza Faria

Research conducted by the University of Lincoln found that professional soccer players are more likely to be mentally tough; they confront challenges and experience stress differently. Others do not intimidate them; they can handle criticism better, possess a commitment to learning and improving, and are more compliant to instruction (Cook et al. 2014).

My life has always been a series of challenges and I'm psychologically prepared, but this is the biggest challenge of my life.
-Ronaldo Luis Nazario De Lima

I take compliments and I take constructive criticism. Not everyone loves you. It's the way you react as a footballer. I use it all to make me play better.
-Timothy Cahill

Practice On Your Own

It was very difficult. I started when I was seven years old, in my hometown. Since there were no girls who liked football, I played with the boys. After that, I started to play futsal with the school team and participated in tournaments in nearby cities. Later, at age eleven, I started playing CSA de Dois Ranchos, in Alagoas.
-Marta Vieira da Silva

Daniel Coyle, who wrote *The Talent Code: Greatness Isn't Born. It's Grown. Here's How* (2009), discussed the importance of playing

Futsal to improve one's soccer game. In his book, he says that every great Brazilian player has played Futsal. The game, which is played on a smaller field with heavier balls, gives players more time on the ball then they would receive in a soccer match. This additional time on the ball helps them practice skills.

Simon Clifford, a coach, went to Brazil to study the game of soccer there, and to understand the formula Brazil uses to produce so many good players. Winning five World Cups and producing 900 or so young players signed to European clubs is no stroke of luck. Also Pelé, Zico, Socrates, Romario, Ronaldo, Juninho, Robinho, Ronaldinho, and Kaka all hailed from Brazil.

Clifford returned to England and established the International Confederation of Futebol de Salao, developing a soccer program based on the observations of teams training in Brazil. He established the club in a rough, impoverished area. He played samba music while they practiced. People laughed at him; however, his under-fourteen squad defeated the Scottish national team and he has one player, Micah Richards, who plays for the English national team.

It is estimated that players touch the ball 600 percent more often with Futsal. Other differences that separate Brazilian players from the rest are that they more often come from backgrounds of poverty, their climate is different, their passion more intense, and the fact that soccer academy players play 20 hours a week verses five hours a week in Britain. Clifford also saw the desperation in the players' eyes.

Scientific research has concluded that it takes an average of eight-to-twelve years of training for a talented player to reach elite levels. This is called the ten-year or 10,000 hour rule, which translates to slightly more than three hours of practice daily for ten years (Ericsson, et al, 1993; Ericsson and Charness, 1994, Bloom, 1985, Salmela et al.,

1998). However, the range of mastery time is between 7,000 and 20,000, depending on the person. Science has found that some people learn some skills faster than others; however, one thing is clear: a long-term commitment is required to produce elite athletes.

Nick Humphries went from an average player at 16 to being offered a contract and playing professionally within two years. Here are the six steps he suggests: give up playing FIFA; create a personal training schedule; work on your weaknesses; read books like *The Outliers* (2011), *The Talent Code* (2009), and *The Gold Mine Effect* (2013); if you make a mistake, rather than getting frustrated, write it down and work on ways to correct it; and finally, be patient and realize that achieving your goals will take months and years of practice with a target of 10,000 hours in order to achieve mastery. At 22, Nick was still pursuing his dream.

I start early, and I stay late, day after day after day, year after year. It took me 17 years and 114 days to become an overnight success.
-Lionel Messi

To watch people push themselves further than they think they can, it's a beautiful thing. It's really human.
-Abby Wambach

Every athlete's natural inclination is to want to practice what he or she is best at, because that's what's the most fun and brings the satisfaction of feeling most successful. A good coach insists that his or her athletes face their fears, shore up their shortcomings, and practice whatever parts of the game they like least, probably because they fail most often there.
-Michelle Aker

The kind of mentality I'm talking about is rare. Not a lot of people have it. They are the ones who do more, go harder, push past, and go after an invisible standard only they can see. It separates the good from

the great and the great from the best. It is relentless. Day in and day out, never diminishing. Twenty-four/seven it is there and takes a back seat to nothing. Injury, disappointments, loss, nothing gets in the way. All obstacles and challenges, in fact, fuel the fire and become an unexpected added dimension of strength and ability along the way. The mentality to excel, to dominate, to do whatever it takes is the mentality born and built in a champion. It is the difference
-Michelle Aker

The vision of a champion is someone drenched in sweat, at the point of exhaustion when no one else is watching.
-Anson Dorrance

My full focus over the years has always been on my career in football. I've always worked hard …it's always been about hard work and I've taken that from the soccer field to the business side of my life. I think that if you work hard in life things happen.
-David Beckham

We're a great team. We can play this game, and we've got a lot of naturally talented athletes who are ready to work to be better.
-Abby Wambach

Commuting in old cars, in winter storms in minus 20 degrees just to go to practice, 150 clicks away, back and forth. I've done that; all winter long in snow and ice and terrible gravel conditions. I think it's good to have that background, because it makes you realize you cannot go to the top if you do not have some tough days.
-Even Pellerud

Even Pellerud (2005) who coached Canada, Trinidad and Tobago, and Norway women's teams stressed the importance of practicing skills everywhere, to refine them, and develop precision. Parents might say their son wants to be a professional soccer player but he has either not touched the ball for two weeks or he practices 20 minutes on a

Saturday, and he's too busy on the internet, using Instagram or Facebook. Parents have to make decisions about where to put their resources, and when they only see their children practice with the team, it's hard to justify the financial sacrifices and time investment parents make. If you want to play professional soccer, there is no way around it: you have to practice on your own.

The secret of the team's success is easy, unity and hard work.
-David Beckham

Researchers have been studying successful people for many years, trying to understand the difference between average people and individuals who achieve mastery. Neurobiology scientists found that when people practice a skill deeply, it changes their brain. The myelin, which forms around the brain and spinal cord to transmit electrical impulses along the nerve cells quickly and efficiently, is more developed in the brains of those who practice longer hours and have deeper practices. For example, they would be faster in assessing why they made a mistake before trying again.

Hard work is a key to achieving success. Professional soccer players have made the sacrifice, spending many hours alone perfecting their skills. Though it's not just the amount of hours spent, but rather practicing effectively. Daniel Coyle, author of *The Talent Code* (2009), studied highly successful people and found that they practice differently. They were average people who, when they made mistakes, stopped and thought about what they did before they tried again. Additionally, they operate to enhance their ability, practicing beyond their current skillset.

I've always watched the players who had the best performance and realized one thing: what makes the difference between good players and stars is the work.

The difference between good players and best players can be in those details.
-Cristiano Ronaldo

Be Willing To Work Hard

Success is no accident. It is hard work, perseverance, learning, studying, sacrifice and most of all, love of what you are doing or learning to do.
-Pelé

I've always really just liked football, and I've always devoted a lot of time to it. When I was a kid, my friends would call me to go out with them, but I would stay home because I had practice the next day. I like going out, but you have to know when you can and when you can't.
-Lionel Messi

One research study found that of the 410,982 high school student athletes, 5.7% went on to join the National Collegiate Athletic Association (NCAA), and 1.9% of those on the NCAA went on to play at the professional level; and of those who were high school athletes, .09% made it to the level of professional soccer. It is clear that hard work is a necessary component for success (NCAA, 2013).

I didn't want to be the rebel who was bottom of the class, so I worked hard. They wanted me to stay on for A-Levels, but football came calling – that was my real love.
-Frank Lampard

It was my father who taught us that an immigrant must work twice as hard as anybody else – that he must never give up.
-Zinedine Zidane

I worked all my life for this.
-Diego Maradona

I know I am extraordinarily lucky to be doing what I am doing. I have worked hard along the way and I have been blessed too. I have had a great life.
-Gary Lineker

But the only person who can truly make you better is you. You have to be willing to accept the information, you have to be willing to work hard; you have to be motivated to go to practice with an open mind. You have to be willing to be criticized. Only you can do those things. And to learn, you have to be willing to push yourself.
-Brandi Chastain

My full focus over the years has always been on my career in football. I've always worked hard and I've always known what works so my career has always been about ... hard work and I've taken that from the soccer field to the business side of my life. I think that if you work hard in life things happen.
-David Beckham

Be Willing To Sacrifice

Success is no accident. It is hard work, perseverance, learning, studying, sacrifice and most of all, love of what you are doing or learning to do.
-Pelé

Those days were the worst of my life. You're 500 kms away, you're without your family. You're from a small place where you can walk everywhere and the change is huge. There were lots of nights I thought: 'I want to go home;' Very hard moments. I'd think I was never going to make it. But you have to be strong. Even at the age of 12 you think: I have to fight. I've come this far, there's no going back.
-Andrés Iniesta

You have to fight to reach your dream. You have to sacrifice and work hard for it.
-Lionel Messi

Researchers from the University of Agder found that football players' level of sacrifice for the team was related to their perception of their coach's leadership. Leadership behaviours such as training and instruction, positive feedback, social support, democratic and autocratic behaviour were assessed. Personal sacrifice was more likely when the coach was perceived as having provided positive feedback. This was the only behaviour that appeared to influence players' level of personal sacrifice in this study (Skjekkeland and Hoigaard, 2009).

To be honest with you, I never looked at soccer as a sacrifice. I think other people may have considered it a sacrifice to miss out on high school dances or do a few high school-type activities. But I always played on my high school soccer team, and I felt very connected in that way so I never felt like I was giving anything up. To be honest, I thought I was always pretty lucky because soccer was what I wanted to do, and nobody told me I couldn't do it.
-Brandi Chastain

It is not sacrifice if you love what you're doing.
-April Heindrichs

Prepare For The Mental Game

Part of my preparation is I go and ask the kit man what colour we're wearing – if it's red top, white shorts, white socks or black socks. Then I lie in bed the night before the game and visualize myself scoring goals or doing well. You're trying to put yourself in that moment and trying to prepare yourself, to have a memory before the game. I don't know if you'd call it visualizing or dreaming, but I've always done it, my whole life.

-Wayne Rooney

Jim Taylor, sports psychology professor at the University of San Francisco, believes that mental imagery is one of the most important components of the mental game. He says that some athletes, when they begin to use imagery, often cannot see themselves successfully completing the task because they do not have confidence in their ability. He suggests recreating the image until you picture yourself succeeding, so that a sense of achievement is ingrained.

When imagining success, do not just use visual senses, but also hear what success sounds like: hear people calling your name after you score a goal, make a good pass, stop a potential goal, or win the ball from your opponent. Begin by slowing down the visualization of the performance to see all of the steps necessary to achieve the required goal and then increase the speed to real time. Imagine the real environment you play in. Is it raining or snowing? Be consistent in practicing imagery as you would practice the technical game, so too should the mental game be practiced regularly, about 3 to 4 times a week. Begin practicing for realistic goals and when you have accomplished them, continue to practice towards reaching more and more challenging ones. You can keep an imagery journal to record what you worked on and practiced.

Stay Motivated

Always have something to look forward to. Whatever it is. If you don't have that, you lose interest, you become stale.
-David Beckham

Most of the professional soccer players seemed very motivated due to their passion for the game. However, at times, there may be a lot of adversities to overcome. It is important to find a way to stay motivated if you temporarily become discouraged. A survey of 3,900 youths in grade 7 to 12 gave the following reasons to participate in sports among boys: to have fun; to do something they are good at; to improve skills; for the excitement of competition; to stay in shape; for the challenge of competition; to get exercise; to learn new skills; to play as a team; and, to get to a higher level of competition.

For the girls, the motivation is similar: to have fun; to stay in shape, to get exercise; to improve skills; to do something they are good at; to learn new skills; for the excitement of competition; to play as part of a team; to make new friends; and, for the challenge of competition (McGroarty, 2014).

Motivation is not something I struggle with. I love playing football, I love being in training, the day-today life is fantastic.
-Lionel Messi

Overcome Differences In Ability

People usually think I was trying to make a statement by playing soccer with able-bodied people and not giving up, but really... I just love playing soccer.
-Nico Calabria

Soccer is a game that can be enjoyed by everyone, including those with physical or mental impairments. Nico Calabria was born with one leg, but when he was five he played soccer on a regular team. He is one of the youngest players currently playing on the U.S. National Amputee Soccer team. In his first US National Team game, he scored a goal against Mexico to achieve a 2-1 win.

I've got one leg, you get one life and do what you will; I'm not going to let the hand I've been dealt with in life dictate what my life is going to be.
-Nico Calabria

I look at disabilities as differences in ability... There's an important distinction. The definition of disabled is basically a long list of synonyms that don't describe me like crippled and weak.
-Nico Calabria

Do Not Give Up

United could soon overtake Arsenal as the chief threat to Chelsea. We will keep fighting to the end. We are Manchester United; that is what we do.
-Roy Keane

You will go through tough times; it's about getting through them.
-David Beckham

We had quite a few good, young players in the school. So I don't think I was the best in the class. I don't think I was best in the school and so for some reason I always remember being picked last in the school games on the field at break time.
-David Beckham

Roberto Baggio played in the FIFA World Cup in 1990, 1994, and 1998 as a striker. He scored 108 of 122 penalty shots in his career. In 1993, he was FIFA's Player of the Year. However, in the 1994 World Cup final, he narrowly missed the net in a scoreless match. He was profoundly affected by the missed shot, stating, "*It affected me for years. It is the worst moment of my career. I still dream about it. If I could erase a moment, it would be that one.*" Four years later, in the 1998 World Cup game, he scored two goals. He never gave up.

The more difficult the victory, the greater the happiness in winning.
-Pelé

The goals you set for yourself, as an individual and as a team become more ambitious and achieving them is all the more gratifying.

-Mia Hamm

Play Fair

An important aspect of football is trying to behave and trying to play fair. Not everyone does this in any walk of life, but I think it's about handling things, learning not to get provoked and not reacting in the wrong way.

-Gary Lineker

Gary Lineker played from 1978–1994 for England's National Team, Leicester City, Everton, Barcelona, Tottenham Hotspur, and Nagoya Grampus Eight. Throughout his entire career, he did not get one caution, yellow or red card. Pelé said he was an example to children worldwide. He holds the records for goals in the World Cup scoring 10. In 1990, he was awarded FIFA's Fair Play Award. In his 16-year career, he played

567 competitive games, and scored 282 goals at a club level and 48 goals at an international level for a total of 330 goals. He was inducted into the English Football Hall of Fame, and was the winner of the 1986 Golden Boot award.

Win or lose, do it fairly.
-Knute Rockne

Find Your Passion

Obviously football is my sport. It's a passion, it's part of my life and I love it.
-Gary Lineker

Georg Hegel, a philosopher of the late 1700s stated in his book, *Reason in History,* that *"nothing great in the world has ever been accomplished without passion."* It was obvious when reviewing soccer interviews for comments on passion that the large majority of players and managers love soccer and their jobs. Some stated they were not working just for the money but for a love of the game. Of the 11 quotes found which could fall into this category, only one did not convey a passion for soccer. Researchers have found that passion for a sport is a predictor of deliberate practice and that practice was a predictor of performance (Vallerand, et. al 2008). Here's what the professionals had to say:

Some people tell me that we professional players are soccer slaves. Well, if this is slavery, give me a life sentence.
-Bobby Charlton

I have a very important role when it comes to defending corners, free kicks and set pieces. I love to do it, too. It gives me a buzz when I clear a corner with a nice header and then we launch a counter-attack. I'm not a player who only thinks about scoring goals – I want to give football more than that. Football has so much more to offer than just goals.
-Robin van Persie

Real Madrid is the most important thing that happened to me, both as a footballer and as a person.
-Zinedine Zidane

To be honest, I've never thought about what I could get out of football or where it would take me. I just wanted to play. I'm the same now.
-Thierry Henry

Money is not a motivating factor. Money doesn't thrill me or make me play better because there are benefits to being wealthy. I'm just happy with a ball at my feet. My motivation comes from playing the game I love. If I wasn't paid to be a professional footballer, I would willingly play for nothing.
-Lionel Messi

As a kid, you obviously dream of being a professional footballer. I would watch players like Ronaldo of Brazil and pretend to be him in the playground. But I don't think about trying to become one of the best in the world or anything like that. I just play football.
-Gareth Bale

I have the chance to do for a living what I like the most in life, and that's playing football. I can make people happy and enjoy myself at the same time.
-Ronaldinho de Assis Moreira

Some people believe football is a matter of life and death. I'm very disappointed with that attitude. I can assure you it is much, much more important than that.
-Bill Shankly

I love soccer but more than playing there's also the audience, the fans — the response I get. They always push me to love and play more and more.
-Marta Vieira da Silva

I don't believe skill was, or ever will be, the result of coaches. It is a result of a love affair between the child and the ball.
-Manfred Schellscheidt

Football has always been my great love; I slept with a ball – really!

-Robin van Persie

I'm just a person that loves my job that is football, and I want to keep enjoying.

-Javier Hernandez

Many professional soccer players express their love of soccer. However, not all soccer players reserve a deep and profound passion for the game. Hytner, in an interview with *The Guardian* (2010), reported on Benoît Assou-Ekotto's thoughts on football. He quoted him as saying,

"If I play football with my friends back in France, I can love football. But if I come to England, where I knew nobody and I didn't speak English... why did I come here? For a job, a career is only 10, 15 years. It's only a job. Yes, it's a good, good job and I don't say that I hate football but it's not my passion. I arrive in the morning at the training ground at 10:30 and I start to be professional. I finish at one

o'clock and I don't play football afterwards. When I am at work, I do my job 100%. But after, I am like a tourist in London. I have my Oyster card and I take the tube. I eat."

Benoît Assou-Ekotto was born in 1984. At 31, his contract with the Tottenham Hotspur was terminated in February 2015. Currently he plays for Saint-Étienne. At the same age, born on February 5, 1985, Cristiano Ronaldo said:

First, it is my life. Second, it is a job that I love. Without football, my life is worth nothing. I want to consistently play well and win titles. I'm only at the beginning. My dream is to win titles again, as I did playing for Manchester United.

Cristiano Ronaldo has almost four years until his contract runs out with Real Madrid and he dreams of continuing his career.

I hope to finish my contract with Real Madrid at 33 and after that we'll see if they want me to stay. I feel

young and still a long way off retiring. Being the best in Portugal isn't enough for me, I'm going to work to be the best ever. I don't have to prove anything to anyone, just to myself. I want to continue working in the same way because it's harder and harder to improve my figures.
-Cristiano Ronaldo

From day one he had the flash and the flare but there was always something there and his work ethic was second to none, it really was. That is the one thing I tell everyone who is around him... his work ethic is incredible. On the ball, in the gym, eating the right food. You know, I just remember every day after training it was always the same. ... It is no secret then. It is no surprise that is how he has ended up. Not everyone does that. He is incredible.
-Tim Howard talking about Cristiano Ronaldo.

Have Fun

I look at Messi, and he makes me laugh. A beautiful footballer who is still like a kid. A world

superstar but still a kid, innocent, you know. He just plays.
-Johan Cruyff

Sebastian Giraldo (2013) found in his doctoral research that play was the missing ingredient in American elite soccer. Too often young people are not allowed to "play" and make mistakes in soccer. He thinks that in the United States, soccer players are not able to think creatively because they have not been afforded the opportunity to play and learn from their mistakes

I have fun like a child in the street. When the day comes when I'm not enjoying it, I will leave football.
-Lionel Messi

Work With The Team

The main thing for me was to win the league. Even if I'd have scored half the number of goals and we'd won the league, I'd still have been happy. The Golden Boot would be like a bonus. In a way, it's

not an honest award - even if you end up with the most goals in a season, those goals are the team's goals and many will have been made possible by other players. They should make a Golden Boot for the whole team.

-Robin van Persie

Luis Amaral, a researcher at Northwestern University, designed a research project and Josh Waitzman designed software to measure every football player in the 2008 European Cup. Together they determined that the individual strengths of the best players complement the team's performance and that there are players who fight for the ball and make precise passes rather than tricks.

I don't like to talk about only me because this is a group game; it's not like tennis or golf with only you playing, you're there for your teammates and working hard for the team is the most important thing.

-Javier Hernandez

Inspiring Stories

Michelle Akers Practices Things She Does Not Enjoy And Fears

Every athlete's natural inclination is to want to practice what he or she is best at, because that's the most fun and brings the satisfaction of feeling most successful. A good coach insists that his or her athletes face their fears, shore up their shortcomings, and practice whatever parts of the game they like least, probably because they fail most often there.
-Michelle Akers

Michelle Akers was born on February 1, 1966, in Santa Clara, California. Like many great female football players, she began playing with the neighbourhood boys. Her interest continued, and while playing for the University of Florida soccer team she was the top goal scorer. Her international career started in 1985 when she scored fifteen goals for the U.S. team in just 24 matches. This was an impressive performance. Despite suffering from chronic fatigue syndrome, she worked hard on her game and led the U.S. to victory in the 1991 and 1999 Women's World Cup Tournaments. After her diagnosis, diet and training modifications, as well as a change from forward to midfield position, made it possible for her to continue to play the game. Mia Hamm described her as being the *"toughest women alive ... made of half iron muscle, half iron will."*

Michelle is one of the greatest international soccer players of all time and was honoured by inclusion in the National Soccer Hall of Fame. She was recognized by FIFA in 2000, jointly with Chinese star, Sun Wen, as Female Player of the Century. Michelle has said that players have a tendency to practice what they like and what they are good at. She believes, however, that it is important to practice what you are not good at and what you fear. She co-wrote the book, *The Game and the Glory* (2000), with Gregg Lewis. After her retirement, she dedicated her time to running a nonprofit horse rescue farm and conducting soccer camps.

My style was to play for the moment. I would jump in and I took a lot of physical risks because I couldn't see beyond the moment. That was my strength and my weakness. I was either going to crash or celebrate big time.
-Michelle Akers

If I go on vacation once or twice a year and have enough money to buy soccer shoes, I'm happy.
-Michelle Akers

David Alaba Plays Fair

I'm living a dream. I wake up every morning and think to myself; wicked, it doesn't get any better. I'll always be grateful to all the people who have supported me.
-David Alaba

David Alaba was born in Austria on June 24, 1992. As a left-back and mid-fielder, he was signed to Bayern Munich at the age of 16, and to the Austrian national football team at the age of 17. During his football career, David has had to overcome many challenges, resulting from injuries as well as racism. Despite all these obstacles, David has developed a reputation for consistent fair play. Red and yellow cards are given to players by the referee when they commit fouls, and most defenders receive these penalties sometimes. However, David has not received a single card in the last two seasons, and only one yellow card in the season prior. The Austrian footballer plays for the German club Bayern Munich, and also the Austrian national football team. When he made his debut in 2009, as a 17-year-old, he became the youngest player to have played for their senior national team. In 2011, when he was just 19, he was recognized as Austrian Footballer of the Year.

Of course I am really down now, but I have one big goal ahead: I want to be back for the decisive last weeks of the season. I will recover well and then give it full throttle in rehab.

-David Alaba

David is always there. Always! He's an incredible player. He's not afraid of playing football. He's disciplined and always thinks about the team and not just about himself. In David Alaba, FC Bayern have a star for years ahead, an outstanding player, an outstanding human being.

-Pep Guardiola on David Alaba

Pelé Followed His Dream

I've come to accept that the life of a frontrunner is a hard one, that he will suffer more injuries than most men and that many of these injuries will not be accidental.

-Pelé

Pelé, originally named Edson Arantes do Nascimento, grew up poor in Brazil. He had no shoes, no soccer balls, no organized soccer team to play for, and very little money for food. His mother did not want him to play football because his dad, also a professional football player, was injured and struggled to support the family. *"My mother told me, "Don't play football. Your father played and then he got injured and now he can't provide for the family."*

Despite these barriers, when he was about nine, he told his dad he would win the World Cup.

The first World Cup I remember was in 1950 when I was nine or 10 years old. My father was a soccer player ... I saw my father crying ...and I said, "Why are you crying?" My father said, "Brazil lost the World Cup." "Don't cry, don't cry, I'm going to win the World Cup for you." Eight years later, in 1958, I was playing for Brazil when we won the World Cup in Sweden.
-Pelé

He let nothing keep him away from his desire to play soccer and found a solution for every problem life put in front of him. To solve the challenge of not having a ball, he made one out of socks and newspapers. Later, he set up a team on his own by gathering together a group of friends. Then, to acquire a real ball, they began selling peanuts to raise enough money to buy one. They played in the street with the new ball, but still could not afford shoes, so like many Brazilian street teams they played without them. When he became good enough, many teams wanted him to play for them. Santos FC hired him when he was only 15 and he went on to play for Brazil.

Throughout his career, Pelé often discussed his spiritual belief that soccer was a God-given gift and a responsibility. He inspired the Brazilian team to pray before the World Cup. In his autobiography, Pelé talked about the importance of prayer in preparation for the 1970 World Cup, remarking that the team prayed almost daily. Pelé credits the idea of praying before games to his wife Rose, who mentioned that every day the family was getting together to pray. He thought it was a great idea and discussed it with other players who agreed. The prayers were for the victims of the Vietnam War, the sick, as well as for luck and against injury rather than for winning the World Cup. The collective prayer helped with team spirit. When the team had won, Pelé found quiet time to thank God. Religion always played an important part in Pelé's life. He used to go to church before every game when he was young. He also felt strongly that God gave him a gift and that he had a responsibility to utilize it for good things. Pelé believes that everything he has done, he owes it to God and that his faith has helped him throughout his life (Pele, 2015).

Pelé played at Santos for most part of his career. After his retirement, he was recruited to play for the New York Cosmos. They believed that his international fame would increase interest in

American soccer. In his career, he won three World Cups for Brazil and scored 1,283 goals in 1,367 games. Pelé received an honorary Ballon d'Or when he was named FIFA Player of the Century in 2000. He was also a global ambassador for soccer. Pelé, like many other players, believed a career in football was possible for him.

"Are you crazy! We can't play there. There's a civil war going on there." But the organizers said, "No, no, the people want to see Pelé play. We are going to stop the war to see Pelé play." So they stopped the war for forty-eight hours and they got to see Pelé play.
-Pelé

David Beckham Overcomes Adversity

I just want people to see me as a hard-working footballer and someone who is passionate about the game.
-David Beckham

David Beckham was born in London, England on May 2, 1975. When he was around nine, he was determined to be a football player and believed it was possible for him to achieve. He practiced hard with a strong focus on his dream, and by 14 he had signed a contract with Manchester United, his favourite team. While Beckham received a lot of honours, he made a mistake, which he acknowledged too, of kicking an opposition player. This resulted in a penalty kick, which some felt made England lose its chance of winning the 1998 World Cup. Some fans began to bully and threaten him. He even had to have police escort him to games on occasions. This was one of the most difficult times of his life. But he continued to play soccer and, in 2002, he scored a goal in the World Cup to help England win, which won him back the support of fans.

In the last 10 years I've probably been through a lot of ups and downs in football and in life and I've come out of it. I'm still England's captain, playing

for one of the biggest clubs. I'm married. I've got three (now four) beautiful kids; life could not be better but I know having been through it a few times.
-David Beckham

Sir Alex Ferguson commented about David Beckham in an interview for Express (2013) saying, "*He lost the chance to become an absolute top-dog player. He wanted to give it all up for a new career, a new lifestyle, for stardom... The big problem for me ... he fell in love with Victoria. And that changed everything.*" What defines success? Financially, David Beckham is estimated by Celebrity Networth to have an annual salary of $50 million and a net worth of $350 million, and is considered to be one of the world's richest athletes. He began playing professional soccer at 17 and played nine years for Manchester United, achieving a childhood dream. He went on from Manchester to play for Madrid Real, LA Galaxy, and played for England's National Team. After a 21-year soccer career, he retired having won 10 league titles. His commercial sponsors included Adidas, Coty,

H&M, Sainsbury's, Samsung, and Breitling. He is an ambassador in China, still playing exhibition games. Currently, he hopes to buy an MLS team. In 1999, Beckham married Victoria Adams of the Spice Girls and is still married. He has four children – three boys and a girl. He is a model, ambassador, and businessman. I think many people would consider him a success. Below are some words of wisdom from the man himself.

I want to carry on playing for the country and leading England as much as possible. I would love to get to the Bobby Moore, Bobby Charlton's record of caps. I'd love to reach that – I know I'm going to miss football once I finish but I know I'm going to make sure I have things outside of football that are going to keep me busy.
-David Beckham

...so many moments in my career and so many moments in my life where I look back and I think I wanted to play for Man United; I wanted to play at Wembley. I wanted to captain my country and it is

just incredible to me to just look back and see this is what I dreamt of as a young kid and whatever you think, whatever you want, whatever you dreamt of as a kid, those things can happen, whatever you want those things can come true.
-David Beckham

At the end of the day, I'm a footballer who has played at some of the biggest football clubs in the world and played with some of the best players in the world.
-David Beckham

Nico Calabria Lets Nothing Stop Him

My parents always instilled in an attitude of, "Hey, tough luck, man. You were born with one leg. Now make the best of it."
-Nico Calabria

Nico Calabria was born with one leg, but this has never stopped him from achieving his goals. At three, he made the decision to discard the prosthetic leg and opted for crutches. By the age of five, he was playing soccer on a regular team. He soon became one of the youngest players to be selected for the US National Amputee squad. He proved his abilities in the first game with the National Team, when he scored a goal against Mexico to achieve a 2-1 win. Nico does not view soccer as a short-term goal, *"I'm planning on being a part of the team for the rest of my life, until I can't play anymore. I have another 25 to 30 years ... as long as my body can keep up with it."* He is very appreciative of his parents' support and feels their tough love attitude helped him.

From a young age I had to struggle with being different and my parents wouldn't exactly console me. They would make it clear that there was nothing to do that could change my situation. I could only live life to the fullest.
-Nico Calabria

It was hard sometimes, but my family always had a 'no excuse, tough love mentality' when it came to overcoming challenges.
-Nico Calabria

In addition to achieving his soccer dream, he was also the youngest person to ever reach the summit of Mount Kilimanjaro and the first on crutches. In doing so, he raised over $100,000 for the Free Wheelchair Mission, which provides wheelchairs at no cost to people in the developing world. This money enabled the purchase of 2,000 wheelchairs for people in Africa. Calabria's daring act was documented in a 15-minute film called, *Nico's Challenge*. The film won first place at the American Pavillion Film Festival in Cannes, France. It won many other awards. Nico appeared on popular TV shows like *The Ellen DeGeneres Show*, and radio sessions such as National Public Radio's *All Things Considered*, and was also a speaker at the Mountain Film Festivals in Colorado and Vermont. He has received an Outstanding Wrestler award, the Ambassadors of

Mobility Award from his Free Wheelchair Mission, and the Inspiration Award from Shane's Inspiration. He lets nothing stop him from accomplishing his dreams.

I'm just so lucky to have this international platform to tell my story.
-Nico Calabria

Mia Hamm Works Hard To Improve

I've worked too hard and too long to let anything stand in the way of my goals. I will not let my teammates down and I will not let myself down.
-Mia Hamm

Mia Hamm was born on March 17, 1972. Born with a clubfoot, which required corrective shoes. Once her braces came off, there was no stopping her. As a young child, she moved around a lot because her father was in the military. Often there were no women's teams so she played with the boys' teams, leading the scoring when she was just 11. She was inspired by her brother, Garrett, who helped her develop courage and later by her coach, Anson Dorrance, who helped her believe in herself and improve every day. At just 15, she joined the United States national team. She has described herself as shy, introverted, and Mia felt intimidated by her teammates. In 1997, her brother Garrett died of a rare blood disease. Grief-stricken, she found that playing soccer helped her deal with her sadness.

For the majority of her career, there were no professional female teams. However, Mia was able to play for Washington Freedom a few years prior to retirement. Part of a group of women, who led in the development of women's soccer in the United States, she became an internationally recognized soccer player and was named one of the top 125 FIFA best living players. She held the record for most international goals scored until Abby Wambach scored her 159th. Mia authored, *Go For the Goal: A Champion's Guide to Women's Soccer and Life*, and has also written, *Never Quit*, a book for children. *In Go For the Goal*, she discusses the importance of drive, even when practicing and to always push beyond your limits and that it's difficult to stay on top.

Mia credits many factors contributing to her achievements. Sacrifices are required, including time away from families, jobs, and friends. She discusses the need to do what is best for the team rather than yourself as an individual, suggesting that in the end it might turn out better for you. Additionally, she acknowledges the support of parents and credits her coach, Anson Dorrance, for helping her get better every day, and developing and maintaining her confidence.

Having fun and loving the game provided the motivation to play and practice. Love of competition was also important and she felt this was a defining characteristic of winners and those who achieve top ranks in soccer. Mia believes that mental toughness is the most significant trait. To win against tough competition, you must be able to dig deep down inside yourself to find the drive and power to realize what you thought was impossible. Think in positive terms rather than negative. You need to find the zone; it is one of the hardest things to do in soccer. Mental toughness requires extreme sacrifices. Selflessness is required to make a successful team. You need to put in more hours than other people. That is what makes a champion. Talent and mental discipline often forecast the outcome all other factors being equal. Michael Wilbon, journalist for the *Washington Post*, referred to her as *"perhaps the most important athlete of the last 15 years."*

I've worked too hard and too long to let anything stand in the way of my goals. I will not let my teammates down and I will not let myself down.
-Mia Hamm

Zlatan Ibrahimovic Decides His Destiny

Ronaldo was his idol. I remember we were at Milan, fortunately Ronaldo scores two goals ... and that was happiness for Zlatan to see his idol score two goals and he says "I'm going to be here one day." He wanted to be better and better and I think that is one of the keys to his success; he has always had goals.
-Johnny Gyllenso talking about Zlatan

Nobody believed I could do it. Everybody was trash-talking. They thought I will go away because I have a big mouth. They thought this guy's vision is crazy. It will not happen. But I had these dreams of where I would end up. And now here I am.
-Zlatan Ibrahimovic

Zlatan was born on October 3, 1981 in Malmö, Sweden. His parents were new immigrants to Sweden, and his childhood was tough. In an interview with *Eurosport*, Zlatan described his neighbourhood as a "type of ghetto" and described himself as small as a child. In regard to playing football he said, *"I felt like they had more advantages than me, and I had to be 10 times better than them."* In another interview with Grant Wahl, Zlatan talks more about his feelings growing up. *"I felt I wasn't accepted. But that's maybe what drove me, what gave me the will to do even better, to give me the adrenaline to do even more. So that made me angry to become better. And luckily they didn't make me angry to do stupid things."*

His parents separated and he lived with his mother initially but later moved in with his father. Zlatan remembers his father using rent money to send him to a training camp. He avoided alcohol and drugs, he said, *"I was, maybe, scared [of alcohol and drugs] and so I stayed away. I was different."* In his neighbourhood there were football pitches and he spent a lot of time playing outside. He loved soccer and sometimes, as a young boy, even slept clutching the ball.

In 2015, during a game with Caen, he received a yellow card for removing his shirt after a goal. He had tattooed the names of 50 starving people from around the world, who had been helped by the United Nations World Food Programme. In an interview with *ShortList*, Zlatan discussed food and hunger saying,

Like any top club we have nutritionists and follow a healthy diet, but it's not like they check our refrigerators. When I was growing up we were so poor that our refrigerator was always empty, so now it is a rule in our house to always have it full. I am not ready to retire for a long time, so I want to look after myself.

His biographer, David Lagercrantz, relates, "*The first time I met him I was nervous because I really wanted to write this book. He asked me, the first questions, 'David, do you believe in God … and I said 'I don't know, Zlatan,' and he said, 'Well you don't believe in Zlatan either because God sent me to Rosengard to play football.'*"

Zlatan has now become an idol to many, instilling a sense of hope and optimism in the possibility of achieving one's dreams. He now plays as a striker for Paris Saint-Germain, and has made over 100 appearances for Sweden.

It's a special thing because he grew up here and it's his court, he has done some good because maybe someone else will play here and be like him. He is very special.
-Child in documentary with *BeIN Sport*

I want to be like Zlatan because he can do a bicycle kick from over twenty meters.
-Child in documentary with *BeIN Sport*

For many kids he is a role model in that way, and that shows that if you really want something it can be done.
-Kent Andersson, Mayor of Malmö

Zlatan means hope for them. They grow up and of course think there is no way for us to get into Sweden society but then they see that Zlatan did. He really means hope. It's possible, it's possible—and that's beautiful.

-David Lagercrantz, Author of *I Am Zlatan*

I think I have changed a lot. You don't have the same body and physical strength. You don't have the same mental strength and thinking. Now, everything depends on me in every occasion but it's not like I am 20. I can't run like I used to then! I play more intelligent today and more complete.

-Zlatan Ibrahimovic

Ibrahimovic also attributes a great deal of his success to a voracious attitude towards training, as well as a courage that comes from a deep passion for the game. When it comes to training, he says talent is not enough. Training hard, practicing all the time, and living healthy are all part of what Zlatan claims are essential, regardless of any player's inherent proclivity. He also claims he was born to play football, and this is part of what gives him the courage to try the unthinkable. Here is a striker that has scored goals that many would think is impossible, and that a lot of players would shy away from in the midst of a high stakes game. Ibrahimovic states he doesn't worry about if it will work every time, and his coaches support the player's brave moves that strive for the spectacular. He has won numerous awards including being named Sweden's Player of the Year nine times.

It's up to me. So, if I want to become something that I think I can become, I have to train hard. That's my mentality, I like to train hard. I mean, you can have talent, but talent don't take you all the way.
-Zlatan Ibrahimovic

You have to believe that the goals can be scored and not worry about if they will work every time. Some of the goals I have scored have been called unbelievable but maybe it is because many players are not brave enough to try them during a big game. Then, of course, you have to practice – just like with anything you want to be exceptional at. The coaches never tell me off for trying spectacular things as they know what I am capable of.

-Zlatan Ibrahimovic.

If you are different, or you have minimum possibilities, you can still succeed. I am living proof of that. I didn't have that 'wow' life. I was not a 'wow' person. Those around me were not 'wow' people. I didn't live in a 'wow' area. So my message to those who feel different, or unlucky, is that if you believe in yourself you will also make it. There is always a possibility. Everything depends on you.

-Zlatan Ibrahimovic

Philipp Lahm Is A Team Player

When I was a kid, I always dreamed of winning the World Cup and lifting the trophy. That was my dream and you think about that.

-Philipp Lahm

Philipp Lahm has dreamed about winning the World Cup since he was a kid; a goal he would achieve. He has captained both Bayern Munich and the German national team. At 5'7" he was considered one of the best fullbacks in the world. And you could imagine his surprise when his coach wanted him to play in the midfield position, a change many players would not have relished. However, he listened to his coach, asked questions, discussed the idea, and successfully made the necessary transition. In one game, he made 134 passes with a 100% completion rate. *"It was good because it was different. I played at full-back for 10 years and then there was the chance to do something new."*

Philipp does what is right for the team. He is a team player. He won the World Cup, Champions Leagues, and the German League Cup. Lahm is contracted to Bayern until 2018, but has retired from his international career with the national team after winning the World Cup in 2014.

I was convinced we were going to win before the game. I had great faith in the team and I wasn't really worried.

-Philipp Lahm

Four years is such a long time in football. I'll be 34 so we'll have to wait and see. I want to stay in this sport because I love the game and football is such great fun. I definitely want to stay in football but we'll have to see in what capacity.

Philipp Lahm

People forget I'd been playing for Germany for 10 years and that I was in the side for nearly every game and I played in so many tournaments. You're always under pressure when you play. I was never just a player. I wanted to accept responsibility. I've been captain of Bayern and Germany for the past few years. That means not just going on the pitch to train or play for 90 minutes. There's more to it. You want to have an influence, discuss tactics with everybody and deal with everything else involved. You invest a lot of energy in it.

-Philipp Lahm

Lionel Messi Makes Sacrifices

I prefer to win titles with the team before individual prizes or outscoring everyone. I'm more concerned with being a good person than being the best footballer in the world. In the end, when all this is over, what can you take with you? My hope is that when I retire that I'm remembered as a good guy. I like to score goals, but I also like to be friends with the people I play with.
-Lionel Messi

There's nothing more satisfying than seeing a happy and smiling child. I always help in any way I can, even if it's just by signing an autograph. A child's smile is worth more than all the money in the world.
-Lionel Messi

For my part, I try to do my bit to make people's lives more bearable, in particular children across the globe who are having problems.
-Lionel Messi

Lionel Messi was born in Argentina on June 24, 1987. He was noticeably smaller than other children and was diagnosed with a growth hormone deficiency. FC Barcelona youth academy offered to pay for the medication, which his family could not afford. His whole family sacrificed in order to pursue a dream and hope that that perhaps with the medication, Messi might grow tall enough to play football. He moved to Barcelona, Spain when he was 13 and was often homesick for the country he'd left behind. He was described as shy, introverted, and a fussy eater. However, with proper medication and hard work, he is now ranked as one of the best current players world-wide by FIFA.

He has won numerous trophies including four Ballon d'Or. In interviews, he often discusses the importance of being a team player and working hard, making sacrifices, loving soccer, and having fun. He is a role model for youth on how to achieve your goals and dreams regardless of physical challenges. Lionel Messi has a new autobiographical book titled, *Messi: Choose to Believe* (2014) that he wrote to raise money for charity.

I'm lucky to have landed at this Barça where they are excellent players. They have given me everything: the individual awards, the titles, the goals, everything. This team has reserved its spot in history for everything that it has already won. I'm lucky that I get to play here and that I get to play for Argentina, where I get to play with fantastic players. It's so fundamental to be able to play with quality teammates. This team makes me a better footballer, that's for sure. Without the help of my teammates, I would be nothing. I wouldn't win anything. No individual awards, no titles, nothing.

-Lionel Messi

Ronnie has been massively important for me. I was so young when I started to come into Barça's dressing room, but he made a point of being first to step up to me and look after me. I try to copy little things Ronaldinho does, but more fundamentally, I just try

to play for the joy of it. Look at the way he always has a smile — that's how I feel.
-Lionel Messi on Ronaldinho

Alex Morgan Developed Confidence

Keep working even when no one is watching.
-Alex Morgan

Alex Morgan played many sports when she was young and did not start playing soccer until she was 14. Yet she was a first draft pick in 2011, and the youngest player on the U.S. team for the FIFA Women's World Cup. In 2012, she was part of the team that won a gold medal at the London Olympics. Alex credits soccer with giving her confidence.

Every time she joined a new team, she had self-doubt, and this forced her to work through her insecurities. She wrote a series of books called, *The Kicks* to help show young girls the importance of confidence.

She said, "*It is important that, as women, we stand up for ourselves, stand up for our peers, and show the power that confidence can have for women everywhere.*"

I have learned many, many things while playing at Cal, but probably the main thing that players and coaches have taught me is to always work hard, never give up, and fight until the end because it's never really over until the whistle blows.
-Alex Morgan

Ronaldo Overcomes Challenges

Every time I went away I was deceiving my mum. I'd tell her I was going to school, but I'd be out on the street playing football. I always had a ball on my feet.
-Ronaldo Luís Nazário de Lima

Ronaldo Luís Nazário de Lima, famous across the world simply as "Ronaldo," was born in Brazil on September 18, 1976. He grew up in a poor neighbourhood. Ronaldo said, "*I had a very difficult childhood, but I always knew I wanted to be a football player.*" At the age of 12, he was an active member at the Tennis Club Valquerie where he did not play tennis but a type of soccer called futsal. His talent for sports was noticed from an early age, and by the time he was 16, he had been selected for the Cruzeiro team. At a young age he began playing for Cruzeiro where he scored 44 goals in 47 games. As a professional, he suffered a severe knee injury, which forced him to undergo surgery. He was given only a 50% chance of returning to the game.

My biggest motivation is the love that I have for the game of football. It's that love that makes me willing to go through all of this. It will be worthwhile when I play football again.
-Ronaldo Luís Nazário de Lima

Journalist, Juca Kfoui, said, *"I think he's a phenomenon, I think his comeback is the finest example of someone battling against the odds that I have seen, ever, for this boy to do what he did after everything he went through is incredible."* Ronaldo returned from injury and scored two goals in the World Cup final. *"Sometimes I look back and think of when I had the operations, when I was lying in a hospital bed, and blood was pouring from my knee; I think of that time in my life I just have to remember to give me strength."*

Because of the recovery period required, he was not able to return to football for about two years. During this time, he advocated for fair play. Ronaldo has said that it was his passion and love of soccer that kept him going through the sacrifices needed to recover from the knee surgery. He has played in two winning Brazil teams at FIFA World Cups and is recognized as one of the *"Greatest Players of the 20th Century"* by World Soccer.

I always try to have fun despite all the pressure.
-Ronaldo Luís Nazário de Lima

My life has always been a series of challenges, and I'm psychologically prepared, but this is the biggest challenge of my life.

-Ronaldo Luís Nazário de Lima

Manuel Neuer Has A Positive Attitude

I also had a dream [to become a pro player], so I had to give this sacrifice... I'd like to get a part of my youth back. In exchange for that part in which I lived in strict structures at cost of my free will.

-Manuel Neuer

Manuel Neuer was born on March 27, 1986, in West Germany. He worked hard and made sacrifices to achieve the success he has today.

[I] had years where I left the house at 7 am in the morning and returned home at 9 pm in the evening, four days every week. Just like a top manager, but as a juvenile. On Wednesdays I always got home around 4 pm, it was my only day in the week when I had the evening off. On weekends, we had the league

games. It was difficult for the family as well, because I was often not at home. It is difficult to get and keep friends who are willing to cope with that.

-Manuel Neuer

Manuel progressed through his hometown club and signed to work professionally in 2005. When he was 20, he received the honour of starting for Bayern Munich. He currently plays goalie for both Bayern Munich and the German national team. In 2014, he was awarded the Golden Glove for his performance in the FIFA World Cup after he achieved over 1000 sequential minutes in the competition without conceding a goal. He talks about the importance of mental attitude when preparing for the World Cup. *"For a couple months a lot has gone on in my mind. You work up the right attitude for such a long trip, the biggest tournament and the immense heat."*

A key to his success is his focus on attitude, health, and continual skills development. He considers the mental game as the most important part of a successful performance. He said: "*I do not think negatively. I always think positive. If you ponder all the time about what is or could be dangerous, it would kill all the fun.*" Outside of soccer, he campaigned against child poverty and started the Manuel Neuer Kids Foundation.

It is the whole package, my body. I take care that it keeps functioning, that I stay healthy and that I can do everything to improve my skills. But the most important part is the control center, i.e. my head. If that part doesn't work properly, I cannot do the things like the way I intended them to do.
-Manuel Neuer

An inspiring challenge is to repeat success. If a player shoots a ball excellently, so it nets in the far corner, everyone says it was luck. But if the same player is able to repeat this, people gonna say: Hey, he's really skilled at that!
-Manuel Neuer

My ambition is to create some sort of equality of opportunities for children. Everyone can try to help with the resources you currently have. As for me, I can do that at best during my active time, of course, for as long as people show interest in my person.
-Manuel Neuer

If we're not fully concentrated, we can lose games.
-Manuel Neuer

Arjen Robben Makes The Best Of Life

Arjen Robben was born on January 23, 1984 in Bedum, Netherlands. He currently plays for Holland's national team and Bayern Munich. Early in his career, he was diving and sustained injuries.

It wasn't unfair because the statistics don't lie. But now I know the reasons. At the time you hear people say you are made from glass. I was angry because I felt like I was always having to defend myself. I felt strong, a physically strong guy. I was quick.
-Arjen Robben

In 2012, he missed two penalty kicks and suffered an injury, which resulted in him losing his starting position and being a substitute player. *"One of my sad moments in my entire football career is missing a penalty against Chelsea in the UEFA Champions League final in 2012. I was heartbroken and lost confidence,"* Robben said. However, he never gave up and in 2013, he had, what many thought was his best season, scored 21 goals and 17 assists. His achievements and come back are thought to be the result of his attitude and support from his coach. Dominic King interviewed Robben talking about Guardiola,

"In my first conversation with him, he told me it was important I started to enjoy football. He didn't want me to relax but he wanted me to appreciate what was in front of me. He said: 'Enjoy football, enjoy your life.' Straight away he gave me confidence."

During this time, he increased his efforts training even harder at the gym. At 31, he is ranked as one of the top three players in the world and appears to be only improving his game, year after year. Arjen Robben was awarded the FIFA World Cup Bronze Ball in 2014 and the Dutch Sportman in the same year. Arjen Robben is a player who makes the best of what life gives him.

Cristiano Ronaldo Believes In Himself

I never tried to hide the fact that it is my intention to become the best.
-Cristiano Ronaldo

There is no harm in dreaming of becoming the world's best player. It's all about trying to be the best. I will keep working hard to achieve it, but it is within my capabilities.
-Cristiano Ronaldo

Cristiano Ronaldo was born on February 5, 1985 in Portugal. As a child, Ronaldo's life was challenging. His father had died from complications of excessive drinking and his mother had to work. When he was kicked out of school at 14, his mother encouraged him to chase his football dream. At one time, Ronaldo was thought to be too small by the Sporting Youth Academy. But, he continued to practice his ball control and weight training. When people didn't believe in him, he continued to believe in his ability to be the best soccer player, and to this day, he works hard to achieve this. His coaches have said he is a tireless workhorse with a strong work ethic.

His positive mental attitude is demonstrated throughout his interviews. The quotes outlined in this book illustrate a person who has a dream, believes in himself, and has faith, support, and works hard to improve.

Manchester United signed him for £12 million in 2003. He has won many awards including the World's Top Goal Scorer, three Golden Boots, three Ballon d'Or as well as numerous other trophies. He is ranked as one of the best among current players. Having scored over 50 international goals, he is Portugal's best striker of all time.

I want to be remembered as part of the group of the greatest players ever.
-Cristiano Ronaldo

Marta Overcomes Barriers

In the region I come from, it was not acceptable for a woman to play soccer. It was something absolutely masculine. So I really had no options.
-Marta Vieira da Silva

Marta Vieira da Silva was born on February 19, 1986 in Brazil. She had no female role models, and there were no local teams for girls that she could play on. Soccer was not a sport played by many women in Brazil, yet she pursued her dream of becoming a professional footballer. Her ambition was to compete as part of Brazil's women's team against other countries.

I didn't know there was such a thing as professional soccer, but I knew that Brazil had a women's team that competed against other countries, and I wanted to be on that team.

-Marta Vieira da Silva

She first realized her own potential when she stood out as a top player in the boys' teams that she was playing on. *"I have always played with boys since the beginning, and sometimes with boys who were a little older than me – and I noticed that I was always standing out. So when I got to that point, I noticed I was pretty good."* Then, at 14, she took a three-day trip to Rio de Janeiro to try out for the top women's team. Successful, she never returned home, and quit school to pursue her dream of a career in sports. When asked if she was scared to leave home and move to Rio, she replied: *"Why would I be scared? It was in my character to want to achieve my goal, and that was where my goal was. So I had to go there."* She is now considered to be one of the best female soccer players of all time, and has competed for Brazil in three FIFA Women's World Cup Tournaments.

Hope Solo Learns From Her Mistakes

I think it's my personality to overcome things, learn from them and become stronger, both personally and professionally.
-Hope Solo

America's famous goalie, Hope Solo was born on July 30, 1981 in Washington, United States. Her parents divorced when she was young. She credits her father with teaching her to play soccer. While she normally played as a forward, she was encouraged to change to a goalkeeper. She refined her skills under the supervision of former national team goalkeeper, Amy Griffen, when enrolled at the University of Washington. Griffen encouraged her to make her career in soccer.

In high school, I had been the forward who won games. It was a huge mental adjustment to learn that my job was to save games.
-Hope Solo

I was becoming a much better tactical goalkeeper. I learned how to read my opponents' runs toward goal, how to position my defenders, how to see the angle... The intellectual side also made goalkeeping so much more interesting. It wasn't just 90 minutes of waiting for my defense to make a mistake. It was 90 minutes of tactics and strategy. The personality traits that had been shaped by my childhood — resilience and toughness — were assets at the position.

-Hope Solo

Her personal life has been subjected to some public controversy. She was suspended for 30 days from the U.S. Soccer team when her husband drove the team van while under the influence of alcohol. Additionally, she was charged in a domestic violence case that was initially dropped but then appealed. As I write this, the case remains unresolved. This was a difficult time in her life and due to her public profile, it was highly publicized. While undergoing these challenges she continued to pursue her soccer career winning the FIFA Women's World Cup Golden Glove and assisting her team win the FIFA Women's World Cup in 2015.

I want people to realize I am just human. I'm just human and I make mistakes. I want people to be able to forgive me [if] they're willing to do so. I just want to be the best athlete I can be, the best person I can be and I know I have a lot of room for improvement.
-Hope Solo

She has played for the Seattle Reign Football Club since 2013 and has been with the United States National Team since 1996 playing on U16, U19, U21 and the Women's National Teams. As of August 24, 2015, she has had 89 shutouts and is currently one of 10 women shortlisted for the FIFA World Player of Year. Her book, *Solo: A Memoir of Hope,* published in 2012, was a best seller.

Robin van Persie Overcomes Failure

Football has always been my great love. I slept with a ball – really! Even when I started going out with Bouchra – ouha! She must have thought, 'What's this…?' When I was five, I joined a club, Excelsior, the club of Kralingen, in the first division. I was always training. On a free afternoon I did individual work with Aad Putters, my youth trainer. Not with the idea of growing to be a star, but for fun. I didn't want to do anything else.

-Robin van Persie

Robin van Persie is a talented football athlete for Manchester United and the Netherlands national team. Football helped him channel his high energy, which used to get him into trouble at school. He has a strong passion and love for football, leading him to devote a lot of time to practice.

I always want to do better than the season before, that's the aim. I didn't reach that last season because of injuries. It just didn't go the way I wanted it to. I

wanted to score more than 30, in the end I only scored 18 goals which is 12 less and I can't be happy with that because I want to do better.
-Robin van Persie

Failure is one of the most common things that people fear the most. Athletes like van Persie are able to overcome adversities like failure because they have already accepted that failure is a real possibility and eventually, it will happen. When faced with failure, people who have true mental toughness are able to dig deep inside themselves and realize that failure is not something to be afraid of. They take that disappointment and learn from it.

I had a bad game and I'm not happy when I have only 12 touches. The main thing is that I am responsible for that, I feel responsible that I only had 12 or 13 touches no one else. I wasn't happy about that game, I could only blame myself. I had a bad game. Every single game you have to try to get into

the game ... in the end I gave not enough in that game, it was one of those games.
-Robin van Persie

Robin van Persie is lucky enough to be surrounded by people who want to see him succeed. He has a team of players who support him along with his thousands of fans and most importantly, his family. Surrounding yourself with a group of people who will support you is a great mental boost. When you feel like you can't go on any more, the people who support you will be the ones who lift you up and help take you that extra mile.

Before training I was introducing myself to other players but of course we know each other because we have played against each other many times. There were a lot of smiles and jokes here and there. Everybody is very helpful here; it feels like a big family, like I'm used to at Arsenal. I was there for eight years so that's part of my life, it's part of my history. I'm proud of it. Arsenal are a great club and

I have a very similar feeling here. It's very family oriented, from the players to the staff. Everybody's kind and helpful.
-Robin van Persie

With passion, a commitment to training and improving, and support from family and teammates, Robin van Persie has achieved many career achievements such as being recognized as one of the top 10 players of 2014 by FIFA, playing for his national team and achieving Netherlands' all-time top scorer recognition.

I expected him to do something with football on a professional basis… As a little boy he was always busy with the ball, and you could see he was fascinated by it. By five he could already control the ball miraculously. You could see he had a passion and the older he was, the more passionate he became. I always supported him and his two sisters in what they wanted to do. It is very important for the kids to know what they like so they can be happy. If their heart goes out to football, then that is what they should do. I tried to encourage them to develop their talent.

-Josée Ras, Robin van Persie's mother

Abby Wambach Eats Well And Focuses On Fitness

We all have dreams, and if you're out there, and you have a dream, and you want something, and you want something so bad you have got to risk everything. You've got to risk being completely devastated if you don't achieve it and when you fall down you have to get back up.

-Abby Wambach

We just got to believe.
-Abby Wambach

Abby Wambach was born on June 2, 1980 in New York, United States. She was the youngest of seven children and felt that her family played a huge part of her success in soccer; they taught her how to stand up for herself and be part of a team. When she was young, she scored 27 goals in her first three girls' recreational soccer games. She was soon moved to a boys' team to develop her talent. Regarded as one of the best female soccer players ever, Abby scored 183 international goals for the U.S. team and holds the record for the greatest number of international goals scored by any player, male or female. In addition, she has won numerous awards including the 2012 FIFA World Player of the Year, which made her the first American to receive the trophy. She believes that it is important to eat better than others and to focus on your fitness in order to achieve success.

If you want to be the best, you're going to have to train harder, eat better and focus on fitness – even though it's your least favorite part of the game. Don't be afraid to fail. Stop making excuses. Leave nothing in the tank and all that effort will pay off in the end. You'll score a lot more goals in your career, but not one of them will happen without the help of a teammate.

-Abby Wambach

I've always been motivated more by negative comments than by positive ones. I know what I do well. Tell me what I don't do well.

-Abby Wambach

I just know that if I put my courage and my head into any ball served in the box, I'm going to wreak havoc on any defense.

-Abby Wambach

I'm confident in my body and my ability to be able to perform when my time is called. I've done it long enough.

-Abby Wambach

Sun Wen Believed In Herself When The Coach Did Not

My father was a football player, and that was a big influence on me... When I was in primary school, about 10 years old, I began to play football, and I loved it right away.

-Sun Wen

I am not very big or very tall, so I learned to use my brain.
-Sun Wen

Sun Wen was born on April 6, 1973 in Shanghai, China. Her father taught her to play soccer and encouraged her interest by taking her to watch men's matches. Sun Wen pursued her career even when discouraged from it.

My coach said that I did not have the ability to play football. He said I was not very good at it. I did not believe him... It motivated me. I moved to another team, and the coach told me that if I worked hard, I could become a good player. That's why I keep on training hard every day, and I have become a famous football player.
-Sun Wen

It has been hard playing professional football in China because you don't have time to do other things.
-Sun Wen

At the age of 17, she was appointed to China's national team. She played in three FIFA World Cup Tournaments and was awarded the Golden Ball and Boot in 1999. In 2000, she was co-named Female Player of the Century with Michelle Akers. When Gerard Robbins asked Wen what she does in her spare time, she responded, *"There is nothing else but soccer."*

I want to be a model for a lot of the Chinese youngsters. I want to be able to show the young people, and their parents, that there is a future for them. They can follow the same steps and become football players. I can make a difference.
-Sun Wen

George Weah Has Faith

Your parents couldn't even get a good meal for you. Growing up was difficult; you have to go on the streets and hustle. It was crazy. There are tribes in Liberia who have all the facilities and don't let other people make life better for themselves. Through sport,

I got the opportunity to go abroad, to make money to help my parents.
-George Weah

The young boy kept having this dream in which he saw himself playing football and scoring goals, lots of goals. It was God's way of showing him his destiny. And he had to follow that destiny.
-Reverend Myer S. Wesseh talking about George Weah

The story of George Weah is one of inspiration and hope. He was born on October 1, 1966 in the slums of Monrovia, Liberia. Raised by his grandmother after his parents separated, the neighbours often fed George because his family didn't have enough food. As a child, he played soccer with makeshift balls and tin cans, but George dreamt of playing football and scoring goals, and his great uncle believed that God had a destiny for him that he had to follow. In the neighbourhood where he grew up, most of the men did not have jobs.

In the 1990s, his country was in a state of war and there were an estimated 15,000 child soldiers. Yet George had faith in his ability and began playing in the Liberian domestic league in his early teens.

One of his early coaches, Parlee Dixon, describes him as a genius. He remembers that George had always wanted to play for the national team and believed he would. He was seen by a scout for Tonerre de Yaounde of Cameroon and Arsène Wenger signed him immediately. He was 22 at the time. Arsène watched over him, managed his diet, and didn't let him drink. Shortly after, he started playing for the first team.

It was difficult for him considering he didn't speak the language and the training was different. However, he managed the transition. Even though it was a challenge for him, he felt he had to play and his positive attitude helped him through this transition to the professional level as is evident by the following quote: *"I had to do what I had to do. I decided to be strong and play to better the negative image of my country. People were very devastated at home and I could never forget about my country but for just 90 minutes I could make that sacrifice and do it."*

Arsène was very surprised because there was too much pressure and yet I had good games. It made me mentally so strong that I could deal with the problems and try to advance my career in a positive sense.
-George Weah

In 2004, he was voted by the world's top sports journalists as African Player of the Century. He contributed his own money to sponsor the Liberian National Team, which he played for and managed, scoring 13 goals before his retirement. George is grateful for the opportunities that his talent and hard work have provided him with: *"Today I'm sitting at my pool when before I never even had room to sleep. I'm grateful to God and to football."*

I know I have a successful career, a successful life. If I sit and say, 'Look, I have a comfortable life,' and I… just think about myself, I don't think that would be fair. That would be very selfish. Because everything I do in my life is to benefit my people.

-George Weah

These are aunts. They always wanted to beat me when I kicked balls into their houses on the street. We had real respect instilled in us, real respect for our elders. I have come a long way from here. Football has been good to me. Everyone has their destiny but you have to make use of the opportunities. I have spent 15 years at the top of my game. It makes me happy. I love the game. I love scoring goals. But I have always taken it seriously. It is not what the game gives you, it is what you give it. It is what you choose. You've got to work hard and make things happen.

-George Weah

Zinedine Zidane Helps Others

I was lucky to come from a difficult area. It teaches you not just about football but also life. There were lots of kids from different races and poor families. People had to struggle to get through the day. Music was important. Football was the easy part.
-Zinedine Zidane

Zinedine Zidane was born on June 23, 1972, in France. His parents had emigrated from Algeria. Zinedine credits his father for teaching him work ethics. *"It was my father who taught us that an immigrant must work twice as hard as anybody else, that he must never give up."* They lived in a tough neighbourhood where crime, unemployment, and suicide rates were high. At 13, he signed as a junior for Cannes club and was on the elite squad when he was 17. He began playing soccer early and achieved many awards winning FIFA World Player of the Year three times, the Ballon d'Or once as well as the Golden Ball.

At times he has had a hard time controlling his temper and in what was his last game before retirement, he was provoked into head-butting a player and then sent off. Zinedine's response was, *"I apologize to all the children and all the people who saw this gesture because this kind of gesture is intolerable, ...my gesture is unforgivable."* He talked about being provoked three times prior to reacting. Zinedine suggested it was important to punish not just the reaction but also the provoking of such behaviour.

In a long career such as his, there are many moments to remember and one needs to focus on the positive lessons we learn by examining Zinedine's life, like hard work, never giving up, and the ability to apologize for behaviour. He has moved on with his career and is now the assistant coach for Real Madrid. He does much charity work for children, some of which included contributing to building two schools and 16 three-bedroom houses. In a Match Against

Poverty, he stated, *"Everyone can do something to make the world a better place."*

I have won many awards, and I am very happy about this, but I am not the best player in the world.
-Zinedine Zidane

It's hard to explain, but I have a need to play intensely every day, to fight every match hard. And this desire never to stop fighting is something else I learnt in the place where I grew up.
-Zinedine Zidane

Conclusions

Studying the lives of professional soccer players helps us to understand what it takes to be at the top levels. These men and women have overcome all types of personal adversities imaginable, including challenging childhoods, illnesses, injuries, poverty, discouraging coaches, and lack of opportunities due to geography, and gender. Once they did make it to the professional league, the challenges continued and included unfair and unmonitored opponents, resulting in injuries and provocations. They also suffered personal losses or committed mistakes and had to find ways to continue to play. The attitudes of these women and men are very inspiring. We can see through their stories the importance of having a dream, believing in it and making sacrifices; of having families or significant others encouraging and supporting us; and, having faith in a higher power, maintaining health, and developing skills to match players at the highest level. It requires believing in yourself when the coach does and dedication and passion so extensive that you can work through years of physical pain to overcome injuries. The sacrifices are enormous and include leaving communities and families, and dedicating time to the pursuit of your dreams while others around you are enjoying other things. These stories encourage us to believe in our dreams, to keep going, and never quit.

Affirmations

My dreams can come true.

I believe in my ability to achieve my dreams.

I am committed to achieving my dreams.

I have a divine purpose.

I have a destiny.

I strive to do my best every day.

I am optimistic.

I am confident in my abilities.

I have a positive attitude.

I can overcome any discouraging attitudes among the people around me.

I have a desire to win.

I have faith in a higher power.

I can find people who support my dreams.

I strive to improve every day.

I can overcome any challenge.

I practice hard even when no one is watching.

I work hard to achieve my dreams.

I make sacrifices to achieve my dreams.

I mentally prepare for all challenges and games.

I am motivated to achieve my dreams.

I let nothing stop me.

I do not give up.

I play fair at all times in response to any situation.

I am passionate about achieving my dreams.

I have fun.

I am a team player.

Author

Barb Chrysler has a BA in Psychology and English, and an MA in Psychology, from Wilfrid Laurier University. Additionally, she has several years of Ph.D. studies at the University of Waterloo. She coached and managed minor athletic teams for eight years, and has two boys who play sports. She has a compelling desire to help youths believe in themselves.

REFERENCES

Abby Wambach.com. (2015). Retrieved October 27, 2015. http://www.abbywambach.com.

Agnew, P. (1999). Top strikers happy to see God as their savior. The Irish Times. Retrieved. May 31, 2015. http://www.irishtimes.com/sport/top-strikers-happy-to-see-god-as-their-saviour-1.255922.

Akers, M. (2015). Mentality. Retrieved March 11, 2015. http://michelleakers.org/mentality.html.

All Football Players. (2015). Ronaldo Luís Nazário de Lima. Retrieved October 16, 2015. http://www.allfootballers.com/ronaldo-ronaldo-luis-nazario-de-lima/.

American Amputee Soccer Association. (2015). Retrieved October 27, 2015). http://www.ampsoccer.org/meet-team.htm.

Anich, I. (2015). The 18. Messi: Suarez and Neymar are "hard to beat" as best teammates ever. Retrieved

June 5, 2015. http://the18.com/news/messi-suarez-and-neymar-are-"hard-beat"-best-teammates-ever.

Ashour. (2008). Ronaldo Story Behind The Legend – Phenomenon. (2008). Retrieved October 9, 2015. https://www.youtube.com/watch?v=an_pUWB0kto.

Ashour. (2008). Ronaldo Comeback Promo, Interview & Report. Retrieved October 16, 2015. https://www.youtube.com/watch?v=0nCeUjMdX44.

Audette, S. (2009). Nico's challenge. Mezzotint Films. Retrieved October 27, 2015. https://vimeo.com/6701825.

BBC.com. (2014). Cristiano Ronaldo: Real Madrid forward wants new contract. Retrieved October 23, 2015.
http://www.bbc.com/sport/0/football/29925331.
BBC. (2013). Excerpts from "Legendary Interview" by the BBC in 2013. Retrieved January 2015.
https://www.youtube.com/watch?v=0aTP8DGdaOke&feature=youtu.be.

The Beckham by Beckham Interview. Retrieved October 16, 2015.
http://davidbeckhamclassic.com/interview-beckham-by-beckham.html.

BeIn Sports. (2014). Who is Zlatan Ibrahimovic? Retrieved October 27, 2015.
https://www.youtube.com/watch?v=ydjx4h2ULBM.

Beswick, B. (2010). *Focused for Soccer: How to Win the Mental Game.* 2nd Edition. Human Kinetics. Ontario Canada.

Biography.com website. (2015). Abby Wambach. Retrieved October 27, 2015.
http://www.biography.com/people/abby-wambach-21331043.

Biography.com website. (2015). Cristiano Ronaldo. Biography.com. Retrieved August 2, 2015.
http://www.biography.com/people/cristiano-ronaldo-555730#early-life.

Biography.com website. (2015). David Beckham. Retrieved October 16, 2015.
http://www.biography.com/people/david-beckham-9204321#video-gallery.

Biography.com website. (2015). Michelle Akers. Retrieved October 22, 2015. http://www.biography.com/people/michelle-akers-21321911.

Biography.com website. (2015). George Weah. The Biography.com website. Retrieved Mar 15, 2015. http://www.biography.com/people/george-weah-37098.

Biography.com website. (2015). Hope Solo. The Biography.com website. Retrieved October 23, 2015. http://www.biography.com/people/hope-solo-20883135#off-the-fiel.

Biography.com website. (2015). Lionel Messi. The Biography.com website. Retrieved May 2, 2011 http://www.biography.com/people/lionel-messi-555732#king-of-spain-soccer-career.

Biography.com website. (2015). Pelé Biography. The
Biography.com website. Retrieved, Jan 15, 2015, http://www.biography.com/people/pelé-3922.

Biography.com website. (2015). Ronaldo Biography. The
Biography.com website. Retrieved. October 16, 2015. http://www.biography.com/people/ronaldo-9463212.

Biography.com website. (2015). Zinedine Zidane. The Biography.com website. Retrieved May 25, 2015, from http://www.biography.com/people/zinedine-zidane-9541232.

Brodsgaard, S. & Mackin, B. (2005). *Goals and Dreams: Celebration of Canadian Women's Soccer.* Nightwood Editions. B.C. Canada.

Burke, J. (2000). In the court of King George. Football The Observer. The Guardian. Retrieved March 15, 2015
http://www.theguardian.com/football/2000/aug/06/newsstory.sport15.

Canadian Soccer Association. Wellness to World Cup: Long Term Player Development. Retrieved January 15, 2015.
http://www.canadasoccer.com/files/CSA_2009_W2WC_Brochure_EN.pdf.

CANAl+ (2011). YouTube Zidane headbutt interview English. Retreived Oct 10, 2015). https://www.youtube.com/watch?v=6a_2LHzxkZE.

Carlisle Video. (2012. One-legged Soccer Player Scores Amazing Goal! Retrieved October 16, 2015. https://www.youtube.com/watch?v=k2FzJVAHtSI.

Carnegie Council on Adolescent Development. (1992).

U.S. Anti-Doping Agency. True Sport: What We Stand To Lose In Our Obsession To Win. Retrieved October 27, 2015.
http://truesport.org/library/documents/about/true_sport_report/True-Sport-Report.pdf.

Celebrity Networth. (http://www.celebritynetworth.com/richest-athletes/richest-soccer/david-beckham-net-worth/ retrieved January 30, 2014.

Chapman, J. (2013). Sir Alex Ferguson: Victoria stopped David Beckham from being one of the greats. Retrieved January 30, 2015.

http://www.express.co.uk/news/showbiz/438598/Sir-Alex-Ferguson-Victoria-stopped-David-Beckham-being-one-of-the-greats.

Ciaran, K. (2012). Ronaldinho: The Fallen Star. Backpage Football. Retrieved May 7, 2015. http://backpagefootball.com/ronaldinho-the-fallen-star/41485/.

Clark, W. (2014). Kids Sports. Statistics Canada. Retrieved March 12, 2015. http://www.statcan.gc.ca/pub/11-008-x/2008001/article/10573-eng.htm#a1.

Cook, C., Crust, L., Littlewood, M., Nesti, M., Allen-Collinson, J. (2014). What it takes: perceptions of mental toughness and its development in an English Premier League Soccer Academy. *Qualitative Research in Sport, Exercise and Health*, 6(3). Retrieved October 27, 2015. http://www.tandfonline.com/doi/abs/10.1080/2159676X.2013.857708.

Coté, J. (1999). The Influence of the Family in the Development of Talent in Sport. *The Sport Psychologist* 13, 395-417. Human Kinetics Publishers, Inc.

Coppack. N. (2013). RvP: My dream season. Manchester United. News & Features. Retrieved March 26, 2015.
http://www.manutd.com/en/News-And-Features/Exclusive-Interviews/2013/May/robin-van-persie-reflects-on-dream-first-season-with-manchester-united.aspx?pageNo=1.

Daniels, T. (2015). Hope Solo on 'Good Morning America: Takeaways from Interview with Robin Roberts. Retrieved May 3, 2015 from http://bleacherreport.com/articles/2376679-hope-solo-on-good-morning-america-takeaways-from-interview-with-robin-roberts.

Desmarais-Zalob, S. (2014). *First, I'd Like to Thank God: An Exploration of the Relationship Between Top Athletes and Spirituality.* iUniversity. IN.

Diaz, G. (1991). Michelle Akers-Stahl enjoys the quiet life in Oviedo after leading the team to a women's world soccer title. Retrieved October 25, 2015. http://articles.orlandosentinel.com/1991-12-18/sports/9112180147_1_stahl-akers-women-soccer.

Disabled World. (2015). Disabled Football Information. http://www.disabled-world.com/sports/football/ Retrieved January 30, 2015.

Doran, K. (2010). Ronaldo: The Story of El Fenómeno. Back Page Football. Retrieved March 15, 2015. http://backpagefootball.com/ronaldo-the-story-of-el-fenomeno/6908/.

Draper, R. (2014). Philipp Lahm exclusive: World Cup winner on Louis van Gaal, German success and why England will have to wait for glory. Mail Online. Retrieved October 15, 2015. http://www.dailymail.co.uk/sport/football/article-2789339/philipp-lahm-exclusive-world-cup-winner-louis-van-gaal-german-success-england-wait-glory.html#ixzz3ZHW54sZh.

Dweck, C. (2013). Mindset-the new psychology of success. Happiness & Its Causes. Retrieved June 28, 2015. https://www.youtube.com/watch?v=QGvR_0mNpWM.

Ellis, R. (January 2015). Hope Solo suspended from U.S. Soccer Team for 30 days. Retrieved August 12, 2015. http://edition.cnn.com/2015/01/21/sport/hope-solo-suspended/.

ESPN. Dear Abby. Retrieved October 27, 2015. http://espn.go.com/i/otl/20130627_kids/abby.pdf.

ESPN. (2013). Hey, data data –swing. The hidden data of youth sports. Retrieved October 21, 2015. http://espn.go.com/espn/story/_/id/9469252/hidden-demographics-youth-sports-espn-magazine.

ESPN. (2015). Carli Lloyd, Megan Rapinoe, Hope Solo on FIFA World Player of Year Short List. Retrieved October 21, 2015.
Facebook. (2015). Famous quotes by Ronaldo Luis Nazario De Lima. Retrieved October 16, 2015. https://www.facebook.com/notes/football-planet/famous-quotes-by-ronaldo-luis-nazario-de-lima/203779702970170.

Eurosport. (2011). Zlatan Ibrahimovic on childhood. Retrieved August 17, 2015. https://www.youtube.com/watch?v=pfLlrcRC1QY.

FC Bayern München. (2014). Alaba: The Hunger is Still There. Retrieved August 18, 2015.

http://www.fcbayern.de/en/news/news/2014/david-alaba-interview-130314.php.

Fenn, A. (2014). Ronaldo: The difference between good and great is hard work. Retrieved October 15, 2015. http://www.goal.com/en-gb/news/3277/la-liga/2014/04/18/4760125/ronaldo-the-difference-between-good-and-great-is-hard-work.

Fiefield, F. (2011). Sandro: 'I told my brother: I'll be the player we should have both been.' The Guardian. Retrieved July 15, 2015. http://www.theguardian.com/football/2011/apr/02/sandro-tottenham-hotspur.

FIFA.com. (2014). Never too Old. The Weekly FIFA: English Edition (October, 2014). Retrieved October 22, 2015. http://www.fifa.com/mm//Document/AF-Magazine/FIFAWeekly/02/45/52/05/51_EN_Weekly_LowRes_51_en_Neutral.PDF.

FIFA.com. (2015). Classic Players: Michele Akers. Retrieved October 23, 2015. http://m.fifa.com/womensworldcup/classic-players/player=michelle-akers-usa-1329785.html.

FIFA.com. (2009). Lineker, still at the top by Fifa.com retrieved March 6, 2015.

http://www.fifa.com/classicfootball/players/do-you-remember/newsid=1010260/index.html.

FIFA.com. (2014). Neymar: Messi and I dream of the final. Retrieved June 5, 2015. http://www.fifa.com/worldcup/news/y=2014/m=2/news=neymar-messi-and-dream-the-final-2277118.html.

FIFA.com. (2012). Pele: I was born to play football. Retrieved June 4, 2015 http://www.fifa.com/worldcup/news/y=2012/m=2/news=pele-was-born-play-football-1586765.htmlF.

FIFA.com. (2015). Ronaldo. Retrieved October 16, 2015. http://www.fifa.com/fifa-tournaments/players-coaches/people=92699/index.html.

FIFA.com. (2003). Women's World Cup. Sun Wen: A world-class soccer player: All China Women's Federation. Retrieved August 18, 2015. http://www.womenofchina.cn/womenofchina/html1/people/sportswomen/7/6773-1.htm.

Fine, A. H., & Sachs, M. L. (1997). *The Total Sports Experience for Kids*. Taylor Trade Publishing.

Fischer, A. (2013). Copied from Mirror Football. Exclusive Interview with Cristiano Ronaldo: What matters to me? Family, football and money? Facebook. Retrieved August 2, 2015. https://www.facebook.com/notes/cristiano-ronaldo-lovers/exclusive-interview-with-cristiano-ronaldo-what-matters-to-me-family-football-an/214453245259105.

Forbes (2015). David Beckham. Retrieved January 30, 2015. http://www.forbes.com/profile/david-beckham/

Forza Intalian Football Staff. (2011). Legend of Calcio: George Weah. Retrieved October 28, 2015. http://forzaitalianfootball.com/2011/08/legend-of-calcio-george-weah/.

Four Dimensions Football. (August, 2014). 50 Pelé Quotes - "I'm Not Dead! I'm Not Dead! Retrieved August 22, 2015. http://www.4dfoot.com/2014/08/06/50-pele-quotes-im-not-dead-im-not-dead/.

Fox Soccer. (2015). Abby Wambach: 'Putting the crest on every single time means something to me.' (Extended Cut). Retrieved October 21, 2015.

https://www.youtube.com/watch?v=4kmMLNhXiGA.

Galeazzi. G. (2012). Faith and football: An unfortunate pairing. Vatican Inside. Retrieved May 31, 2015.
http://vaticaninsider.lastampa.it/en/world-news/detail/articolo/chiesa-fede-calcio-football-church-faith-fe-11946/.

Gilbert, C. (2008). Playing soccer for God: Brazilian footballers and the Holy Sprit. Spiegel Online. Retrieved. October 16, 2015.
http://www.spiegel.de/international/world/playing-soccer-for-god-brazilian-footballers-and-the-holy-spirit-a-578716.html.

Giraldo, S. (2013). Sebastian Giraldo: Developing creativity in youth soccer players: Three concepts from research. Soccer Thought Soccer Blog. Retrieved July 30, 2015
http://soccerthought.com/sebastian-giraldo-developing-creativity-in-youth-soccer-players-three-concepts-from-research/.

Garcia-Mas, A., Palou, P., Gili, M., Ponseti, X., Borras, P.A., Vidal, J.,, Cruz, J., Torregrosa, M., Villamarín, F. and Sousa, C.. Commitment,

Enjoyment and Motivation in Young Soccer Competitive Players. Universidad de las Islas Baleares (Spain), 2Universitat Autònoma de Barcelona (Spain). Retrieved July 31, 2015. http://www.researchgate.net/publication/47554871 _Commitment_enjoyment_and_motivation_in_you ng_soccer_competitive_players.

Gordon, R. A., & Kane, J. M. (2002). Explanatory style on the soccer field: Optimism and athletic performance. Poster presented at the 3rd annual meeting of the Society for Personality and Social Psychology, Savannah, GA.

Gray, A. (2009). Cristiano Ronaldo Interview Special: who is my toughest opponent? It just has to be Chelsea's Ashley Cole. Retrieved March 17, 2015.
http://www.dailymail.co.uk/sport/football/article-1227024/CRISTIANO-RONALDO-INTERVIEW-SPECIAL-Who-toughest-opponent-It-just-Ashley-Cole.html.

Güell, R. (2015). Leo Messi, top scorer and top assister in the Champions League. FC Barcelona website. Retrieved June 16, 2015.
http://www.fcbarcelona.com/football/first-

team/detail/article/leo-messi-top-scorer-and-top-assister-in-the-champions-league.

Hanton, A. (2014). Pele was so good at soccer that he stopped a war. Knowledge Nuts Retrieved March 4, 2015.
http://knowledgenuts.com/2014/10/14/pele-was-so-good-at-soccer-that-he-stopped-a-war/.

Harrison, W. (2015). Soccer players success comes from motivation. Goal Nation: The Voice of Youth Soccer in America – What's Your Goal? Retrieved June 5, 2015. http://goalnation.com/wayne-harrison-soccer-players-success-comes-intrinsic-motivation/.

HBO Sports. (2015). Dare to dream: The story of the US. women's soccer team: Interview with Brandi Chastain. Retrieved April 23, 2015.
http://www.hbo.com/sports/dare-to-dream-us-womens-soccer-team/meet-the-players/brandi-chastain/interview/brandi-chastain.html#/.

Hope Solo. Retrieved August 25, 2015.
http://hopesolo.com/about/.

Hunt, C. (2015). One legged soccer player inspires us all: Follow Nico Calabria's amazing journey to the World Amputee Team. Mens Fitness. Retrieved October 23, 2015.
http://www.mensfitness.com/life/sports/one-legged-soccer-player-inspires-us-all.

Humphries, N. (2014). Fieldo Magazine Why Playing FIFA Will Kill Your Football Career Nick Humphries. Retrieved October 16, 2015.
http://blog.fieldoo.com/2014/01/why-playing-fifa-will-kill-your-football-career/.

Hussey, A. (2004). ZZ top. The Guardian. Retrieved September 10, 2015.
http://www.theguardian.com/football/2004/apr/04/sport.features.

Hytner, D. (2010). Benoît Assou-Ekotto: 'I play for the money. Football's not my passion.' The Guardian. Retrieved June 30, 2015.
http://www.theguardian.com/football/2010/may/01/benoit-assou-ekotto-tottenham-hotspur
http://www.espnfc.us/player/118444/david-alaba?season=2012.

Kerr, J. (2015). USMNT's Bobby Wood interview: 'I didn't insult my coach but laughed when he was fired. The Guardian. Retrieved June 18, 2015. http://www.theguardian.com/football/2015/may/12/usmnts-bobby-wood-interview-i-didnt-insult-my-coach-but-i-laughed-when-he-was-fired.

Kent, D. (2012). Austrian TV channel says sorry to Bayern's Alaba after defender complains of racial insult. Mail Online. Retrieved October 23, 2015. http://www.dailymail.co.uk/sport/football/article-2226986/Bayern-Munichs-David-Alaba-complains-racial-insult-Austrian-TV-channel.html.

King, D. (2014). Tim Howard lifts the lid on Cristiano Ronaldo's obsession with perfection as United States bid to knock Portugal out of World Cup. Retrieved October 16, 2016. http://www.dailymail.co.uk/sport/worldcup2014/article-2664329/Tim-Howard-lifts-lid-Cristiano-Ronaldos-obsession-perfection-United-States-bid-knock-Portugal-World-Cup.html#ixzz3V1ozWxJs.

King, D. (2015). People say Arjen Robben was made of glass at Chelse but the flying winger has won 20 trophies in his career and wants more with Bayern Munich this year. Daily Mail. Retrieved

August 25, 2015.
http://www.dailymail.co.uk/sport/football/article-2985511/People-said-Arjen-Robben-glass-Chelsea-flying-winger-won-20-trophies-career-wants-Bayern-Munich-year.

LeMiere, J. (2014). 50 greatest footballers all time Pele Maradona Messi Ronaldo included in the best soccer in best soccer players ever list. International Business Times. Retrieved October 15, 2015. http://www.ibtimes.com/top-50-greatest-footballers-all-time-pele-maradona-messi-ronaldo-included-best-soccer-1624974.

Jackson, J. (2012). Wayne Rooney Reveals Visualization Forms important Part of Preparation. The Guardian. Retrieved March 16, 2015. http://www.theguardian.com/football/2012/may/17/wayne-rooney-visualisation-preparation.

Independent. (2011). Gary Lineker: It would be hypocritical of me to take payment from MoS Exclusive: This story goes against the national interest because the country is behind the 2018 bid. Retrieved March 15, 2015
http://www.independent.co.uk/voices/commentators/gary-lineker-it-would-be-hypocritical-of-me-to-take-payment-from-mos-1976438.html.

Laurens, J. (2014). ESPN. Talking football, life with Zlatan. Retrieved October 27, 2015. http://www.espnfc.us/blog/espn-fc-united-blog/68/post/1983895/zlatan-ibrahimovic-talks-to-espn-fc-exclusively-about-his-careerthe-champions-league-and-more----laurens.

Lawrence, A. (2000). The wonder of Weah. The Guardian. Retrieved. May 31, 2015. http://www.theguardian.com/football/2000/apr/09/facup.sport.

Lewis, T. (2012). One-legged soccer player and much more. All Around Tim. http://allaroundtim.com/nicolai-calabria-one-legged-soccer-player-and-much-more/.

Loehr, J. (1994). *The New Toughness Training for Sports*. New York, New York: Penguin Books.

Lomas, S. (2015). Barcelona's Neymar – '100% Jesus.' Cross The Line. Retrieved July 31, 2015. http://xtheline.co.uk/neymar-100-jesus/.

New, J. (2015). A Long Shot. Inside Higher Ed. Retrieved July 22, 2015. https://www.insidehighered.com/news/2015/01/2

7/college-athletes-greatly-overestimate-their-chances-playing-professionally.

Nesti, N in Williams, A.M. (2013). *Mental Preparation of Elite Players. Science and Soccer: Developing Elite Performers. 3rd* Edition. Routledge. 2013.

Nzgirl. (2003). 20 Things About David Beckham. Nzgirl. Retrieved from October 22, 2015. http://www.nzgirl.co.nz/buy/2559/.

MacBook Pro Dashboard dictionary.

Mahler, J. (2010). World Cup secrets that raise your game how to get ahead on the field—and off. Shape. Retrieved March 16, 2015. http://www.shape.com/fitness/world-cup-secrets-raise-your-game-how-get-ahead-field-and.

Manchester.com. (2014). The Rooney Files: An Interview with Wayne Rooney. Manchester.com. Retrieved June 10, 2014. http://www.manchester.com/sport/united/rooney-interview.php.

Martin, J. Ed. (2012). *The Best of Soccer Journal: An NSCAA Guide to Soccer Coaching Excellence.* B.O.S.S. Druck und Medien GMBH, Germany.

McGroarty, T. (2014). Inside Youth Sports: Motivation and the Young Athlete (Part 2). Retrieved August 2, 2015. http://www.insideyouthsports.org/2014/08/motivation-and-young-athlete-part-2.html.

Martin, J. Ed. (2012). *The Best of Soccer Journal: An NSCAA Guide to Soccer Coaching Excellence*. B.O.S.S. Druck und Medien GMBH, Germany.

McGroarty, T. (2014). Inside Youth Sports: Motivation and the Young Athlete (Part 2). Retrieved August 2, 2015. http://www.insideyouthsports.org/2014/08/motivation-and-young-athlete-part-2.html.

McRae, D. (2014). Everybody was trash-talking me. Now they're eating their words. That is my trophy. The Guardian. Retrieved August 17, 2015. http://www.theguardian.com/football/2014/oct/06/zlatan-ibrahimovic-trash-talking-sweden-record-golascorer.

Melling, J. (2000). Zizou is the boss now, says Vierira. Soccernet News. Retrieved September 10, 2015.

http://www.espnfc.com/euro2000/news/20000702 finalpreview.html.

Mira, L. (2012). "Neuer: I knew how Cristiano Ronaldo would take his penalty". Goal.com. Retrieved October 16, 2015. http://www.goal.com/en/news/1716/champions-league/2012/04/28/3065829/neuer-i-knew-how-cristiano-ronaldo-would-take-his-penalty.

Munroe-Chandler K, Hall C, Fishburne G (2008) Playing with confidence: The relationship between imagery use and self-confidence in youth soccer players. *Journal of Sports Sciences*. 26(14). 1539-46.

Oden, B. What to do when you hate your coach. About Sports. Retrieved March 9, 2015. http://volleyball.about.com/od/volleyball101/a/Coach-Problems_2.htm.

Pentz, M. (2015). Hope Solo doesn't 'sugarcoat' her past in offering advice. The Seattle Times. http://www.seattletimes.com/sports/reign/hope-solo-doesnt-sugarcoat-her-past-in-offering-advice/.

Pitch International Production. (2012). Ronaldo Luis Nazario De Lima Documentary HDTV.

Retrieved Oct 9, 2015.
https://www.youtube.com/watch?v=-7Ji3uJrtiM.

Potter, S. (2015). Alaba injury reduce Bayersn's options. Retrieved October 23, 2015.
http://www.uefa.com/uefachampionsleague/news/newsid=2230312.html.

Priselac, M. (2014). It Only Takes One Leg To Score A Goal.
http://www.coca-colacompany.com/fifa-world-cup/powerade/it-only-akes-one-leg-to-score-a-goal.
Retrieved January 30, 2015.

Rainbow, J (2013). Messi interview (part one). World Soccer. Retrieved Octoeber 27, 2015.
http://www.worldsoccer.com/features/lionel-messi-interview-part-one-338553.

Rainbow, J. (2013). Lionel Messi interview (part two). World Soccer. Retrieved February 3, 2015.
http://www.worldsoccer.com/features/lionel-messi-interview-part-two-338555.

Ranker. (2015). The best current soccer players. Ranker. Retrieved October 23, 2015.

http://www.ranker.com/list/best-current-soccer-players/ranker-sports?page=2.

Ranker. (2015). The best female soccer players of all time. Ranker. Retrieved October 23, 2015. http://www.ranker.com/list/best-female-soccer-players-of-all-time/ranker-sports?page=2.

Realmadrid. (2015). Ronaldo: Ronaldo Luis Narzario De Lima. Retrieved October 16, 2015. http://www.realmadrid.com/sobre-el-real-madrid/el-club/historia/jugadores-de-leyenda-futbol/ronaldo-luis-nazario-de-lima.

Rice, A. (2005). George Weah's New Game. The New York Times. Retrieved March 15, 2015. http://www.nytimes.com/2005/08/21/magazine/21WEAH.html?pagewanted=all&_r=0.

Robbins, G. (2012). China's Dynamic Soccer Trio. Retrieved August 18, 2015. http://www.lacancha.com/Chinint.html.

Ronaldo7. (2015). Retrieved October 25, 2015. http://www.ronaldo7.net/extra/quotes/cristiano-ronaldo-quotes.html.

Rotella, B., & Cullen, B. (2015). *How Champions Think: In Sports and in Life*. Simon & Schuster, New York.

Sainsbury's. (2014). Video David Beckham Returns to his Primary School After 30 Years. Sainsbury's Active Kids 2014 Equipping Them for a Healthier Life. Retrieved October 16, 2015. https://www.youtube.com/watch?v=G3xzem7HSME.

Schaerlaeckens, L. (2012). Abby Wambach's Interview Outakes. Fox Soccer. Retrieved October 21, 2015. http://blog.foxsoccer.com/post/34858182307/abby-wambachs-interview-outtakes.

Seefeldt, V., Ewing, M., Walk, S. (1992). *Overview of Youth Sports Programs in the United States*. Washington, DC.

SEN Special Education Needs. (2015). Gary Lineker Interview Retrieved March 6, 2015. https://www.senmagazine.co.uk/articles/articles/senarticles/gary-lineker-interview.

Sheen, T. (Oct 26, 2013). Beckham: 'Retiring leaves me with regrets, knowing I'll never play a big match again.' Mail Online. Retrieved May 19, 2015. http://www.dailymail.co.uk/sport/football/article-2477279/David-Beckham-interview-I-feel-pang-regret-I-watch-sport--point.html.

Skjekkeland, V., & Hoigaard, A. (2009). The relationship between perceived coach leadership behavior and personal sacrifice in football. University of Agder Faculty of Health and Sport. The 12th ISSP World Congress of Sport Psychology. Retrieved October 27, 2015. http://www.researchgate.net/publication/265601823_The_relationship_between_coach_behavior_and_personal_sacrifice_in_football.

Sky Sports. (2011). Ronaldo part 1. Retrieved October 22, 2015. https://www.youtube.com/watch?v=ZxZREyWYjlsSky Sports. (2011). Cristiano Ronaldo – Tested to the limits – part 2/4. Retrieved October 23, 2015.

Shergold, A. (2015). Zlatan Ibrahimovic tattooed names of 50 starving people on his body to show support for United Nations World Food Programme before match with Caen. http://www.dailymail.co.uk/sport/football/article-

2954515/Zlatan-Ibrahimovic-tattooed-names-50-starving-people-body.html.

ShortList.com. *(2015)*. <u>Zlatan Ibrahimovic</u>. Short List.com. Retrieved October 23, 2015. http://www.shortlist.com/entertainment/sport/zlatan-ibrahimovic.

Smither, J. W., London, M. (2009). *Performance Management: Putting Research into Action.* Edited by James W Smither.

Soccerbible. (2011). Javier 'Chicharito' Hernandez interview. Retrieved June 5, 2015. http://www.soccerbible.com/football-news/2011/08/javier-chicharito-hernandez-interview/.

Soccerbible. (2012). Wayne Rooney Q & Amp: A – My Time is now interview. Retrieved June 10, 2015. http://www.soccerbible.com/football-news/2012/06/wayne-rooney-q-amp-a-my-time-is-now-interview/.

Soccer TV. Hard Work: 29-year-old Ronaldo reveals the secret of his success. Retrieved July 22, 2015. http://m.livesoccertv.com/news/9693/hard-work-29-year-old-ronaldo-reveals-the-secret-of-his-success/.

Soccerway. (2015). Z.Ibrahimovic. Soccerway Retrieved April 28, 2015.
http://ca.soccerway.com/players/zlatan-ibrahimovic/168/.

Solo, H. (2012). Solo: A Memoir of Hope. Harper Collins.

Sportsmail Reporter. (2012). It was terrible! Robben bemoans miss as Bayern pay price in Champions League final. Retrieved October 22, 2015. www.dailymail.co.uk/champions 2. news.bbc.co.uk/sports2.

Success Story.com. (2015). Ronaldo Comeback Promo Interview. Retrieved October 15, 2015. http://successstory.com/people/ronaldo-lus-nazrio-de-lima.

Pais, E (2012). Leo Messi: I'm more concerned with being a good person than being the best footballer in the world. FC Barcelona. Retrieved June 5, 2015. http://www.fcbarcelona.com/football/first-team/detail/article/leo-messi-im-more-concerned-with-being-a-good-person-than-being-the-best-footballer-in-the-world.

Taylor, J. (2012). Sport imagery: Athletes' most powerful mental tool. *Psychology Today*. Retrieved July 30, 2015. https://www.psychologytoday.com/blog/the-power-prime/201211/sport-imagery-athletes-most-powerful-mental-tool.

Taylor, S. (2013). The power of purpose: Why is purpose so essential for our well-being? Psychology Today. Retrieved July 30, 2015. http://www.ilyke.net/definitely-the-most-kicka-and-coolest-president-in-the-world/44982#RwcFCUQF0U2xKhZI.01.

The Guardian. (2007). Two steps to heaven for Romario as Brazil's old man chases 1,000 goals. The Guardian. Retrieved October 23, 2015. http://www.theguardian.com/football/2007/mar/25/sport.comment2.

The Talks. (2013). Pele My Father and Mother Closed the Machine. Retrieved Jan 15, 2014. http://the-talks.com/interviews/pele/#.

Trans World International/IMB Media . (2010). George Weah – Part 2 . Retrieved May 31. 2015.

https://www.youtube.com/watch?v=SUINYqGEbh0.

Treasure, D. Arizona State University. Motivation is More Than Winning and Losing. Retrieved June 18, 2015.
http://buffalosoccerclub.org/files/pdf/ParentResources/Motivationismorethanwinningandlosing.pdf.

United Nations (2001). French soccer champion Zinédine Zidane to be appointed. Press release. United Nations Information Service Vienna. Retrieved July 20, 2015.
http://www.unis.unvienna.org/unis/en/pressrels/2001/note126.html.

University of Lincoln. (2014). Mental toughness: Why reaching the top in soccer is all in the mind, not the feet. *ScienceDaily*. Retrieved July 21, 2015 from
www.sciencedaily.com/releases/2014/06/140619095847.htm

US Youth Soccer Technical Department. (2008). Youth Soccer in America: How do we measure success? Retrieved February 3, 2015.

http://www.anbfutbol.com/How%20Do%20We%20Measure%20Success%20in%20Youth%20Soccer.pdf.

Verheul, L. (2014). Robin van Persie: I am just a kid with one wish …to play football. The Guardian. Retrieved March 26, 2015.
https://www.theblizzard.co.uk.

Walk Easy Inc. Goooal!. Retrieved October 27, 2015.
http://www.walkeasy.com/interact/stories/nicolai.asp.

Walker, S. (2012). Behaviors that Characterize "Bad Coaching." Podium Sports Journal. Retrieved March 9, 2015
http://www.podiumsportsjournal.com/2012/02/03/bad-coaching/.

Wahl, G. (*2014*). He is Zlatan: 1-on-1 with PSG, Sweden star (and author) Ibrahimovic. Sports Illustrated. Retrieved October 27, 2015.
http://www.si.com/soccer/planet-futbol/2014/06/03/zlatan-ibrahimovic-sweden-psg-world-cup.

Whales, D. (2013). Cristiano Ronaldo, Jose Mourinho bust up: Real Madrid striker says grudges are 'for losers.' Enstars. Retrieved June 18, 2015. http://www.enstarz.com/articles/23088/20130808/cristiano-ronaldo-jose-mourinho-bust-up-real-madrid-striker-grudges-are-for-losers-video-news.htm.

Wikipedia. (2015). Abby Wambach. Retrieved October 27, 2015.
http://en.wikipedia.org/wiki/Abby_Wambach.

Wikipedia. (2015). David Alaba. Retrieved October 16, 2015.
http://en.wikipedia.org/wiki/David_Alaba.

Wikipedia. (2015). Even Pellerud. Retrieved March 11, 2015.
http://en.wikipedia.org/wiki/Even_Pellerud.

Wikipedia. (2014). FIFA Female Player of the Century. Retrieved August 18, 2015
https://en.wikipedia.org/wiki/FIFA_Female_Player_of_the_Century.

Wikipedia. (2015). Gary Lineker. Retrieved August 3, 2015.
https://en.wikipedia.org/wiki/Gary_Lineker.

Wikipedia.(2015). George Weah. Retrieved May 31, 2015. http://en.wikipedia.org/wiki/George_Weah.

Wikipedia. (2015). Hope Solo. Retrieved. October 16, 2015 http://en.wikipedia.org/wiki/Hope_Solo.

Wikipedia. (May, 2015). List of European Cup and UEFA Champions League top scorers. Retrieved June 16, 2015.
https://en.wikipedia.org/wiki/List_of_European_Cup_and_UEFA_Champions_League_top_scorers.

Wikipedia. (2015). Mia Hamm. Retrieved March 11, 2015. http://en.wikipedia.org/wiki/Mia_Hamm.

Wikipedia. (2015). Michelle Akers. Retrieved March 11, 2015.
http://en.wikipedia.org/wiki/Michelle_Akers.

Wikipedia. (2015). Manuel Neuer. Retrieved October 16, 2015.
https://en.wikipedia.org/wiki/Manuel_Neuer.

Wikipedia. (2015). Robert Baggio. Retrieved October 27, 2015.
https://en.wikipedia.org/wiki/Roberto_Baggio.

Wikipedia. (2015). Sun Wen. Retrieved August 18, 2015.
https://en.wikipedia.org/wiki/Sun_Wen_(footballer).

World Soccer. (2008). Ronaldo interview. Cristianoronaldo7.com. Retrieved June 29, 2014.

Van Yperen, N.W. (2009). Why some make it and others do not: Identifying psychological factors that predict career success in professional adult soccer. *The Sport Psychologist*. 23 317 – 329.

Verheul, L. (2014). Robin van Persie: I'm just a kid with one wish…to play football. The Guardian. Retrieved October 27, 20   15.
http://www.theguardian.com/football/blog/2014/may/29/robin-van-persie-kid-one-wish-football.

Zigarelli, M. (September, 2011). The Messiah Method: The Seven Disciplines of the Winningest College Soccer Program in America. Xulon Press. Retrieved June 5, 2015.

http://www.themessiahmethod.com/HowExcellenceHappens.pdf

www.ingramcontent.com/pod-product-compliance
Lightning Source LLC
Chambersburg PA
CBHW020613300426
44113CB00007B/632